Save in 30 days

2$	3$	4$	5$	6$
7$	8$	9$	10$	11$
12$	13$	14$	15$	16$
17$	18$	19$	20$	21$
22$	23$	24$	25$	26$
27$	28$	29$	30$	31$

Notes:_____
_____

Save $500 in 30 days

2$	3$	4$	5$	6$
7$	8$	9$	10$	11$
12$	13$	14$	15$	16$
17$	18$	19$	20$	21$
22$	23$	24$	25$	26$
27$	28$	29$	30$	31$

Notes: _____

Save $500 in 30 days

2$	3$	4$	5$	6$
7$	8$	9$	10$	11$
12$	13$	14$	15$	16$
17$	18$	19$	20$	21$
22$	23$	24$	25$	26$
27$	28$	29$	30$	31$

Notes:

Save $500 in 30 days

2$	3$	4$	5$	6$
7$	8$	9$	10$	11$
12$	13$	14$	15$	16$
17$	18$	19$	20$	21$
22$	23$	24$	25$	26$
27$	28$	29$	30$	31$

Notes: _____

Save $500 in 30 days

2$	3$	4$	5$	6$
7$	8$	9$	10$	11$
12$	13$	14$	15$	16$
17$	18$	19$	20$	21$
22$	23$	24$	25$	26$
27$	28$	29$	30$	31$

Notes:

Save $500 in 30 days

2$	3$	4$	5$	6$
7$	8$	9$	10$	11$
12$	13$	14$	15$	16$
17$	18$	19$	20$	21$
22$	23$	24$	25$	26$
27$	28$	29$	30$	31$

Notes:

Save $500 in 30 days

2$	3$	4$	5$	6$
7$	8$	9$	10$	11$
12$	13$	14$	15$	16$
17$	18$	19$	20$	21$
22$	23$	24$	25$	26$
27$	28$	29$	30$	31$

Notes: _____
_____

Save $500 in 30 days

2$	3$	4$	5$	6$
7$	8$	9$	10$	11$
12$	13$	14$	15$	16$
17$	18$	19$	20$	21$
22$	23$	24$	25$	26$
27$	28$	29$	30$	31$

Notes:

Save $500 in 30 days

2$	3$	4$	5$	6$
7$	8$	9$	10$	11$
12$	13$	14$	15$	16$
17$	18$	19$	20$	21$
22$	23$	24$	25$	26$
27$	28$	29$	30$	31$

Notes: _____
_____

Save $500 in 30 days

2$	3$	4$	5$	6$
7$	8$	9$	10$	11$
12$	13$	14$	15$	16$
17$	18$	19$	20$	21$
22$	23$	24$	25$	26$
27$	28$	29$	30$	31$

Notes:

Save $500 in 30 days

2$	3$	4$	5$	6$
7$	8$	9$	10$	11$
12$	13$	14$	15$	16$
17$	18$	19$	20$	21$
22$	23$	24$	25$	26$
27$	28$	29$	30$	31$

Notes: _____

Save $500 in 30 days

2$	3$	4$	5$	6$
7$	8$	9$	10$	11$
12$	13$	14$	15$	16$
17$	18$	19$	20$	21$
22$	23$	24$	25$	26$
27$	28$	29$	30$	31$

Notes:

Save $500 in 30 days

2$	3$	4$	5$	6$
7$	8$	9$	10$	11$
12$	13$	14$	15$	16$
17$	18$	19$	20$	21$
22$	23$	24$	25$	26$
27$	28$	29$	30$	31$

Notes: _____
_____

Save $500 in 30 days

2$	3$	4$	5$	6$
7$	8$	9$	10$	11$
12$	13$	14$	15$	16$
17$	18$	19$	20$	21$
22$	23$	24$	25$	26$
27$	28$	29$	30$	31$

Notes:

Save $500 in 30 days

2$	3$	4$	5$	6$
7$	8$	9$	10$	11$
12$	13$	14$	15$	16$
17$	18$	19$	20$	21$
22$	23$	24$	25$	26$
27$	28$	29$	30$	31$

Notes: _____
_____

$300 in 40 Days

Savings Challenge

$5	$6	$9	$15	$13
$23	$12	$7	$2	$24
$16	$14	Free	$10	$4
$11	$18	$21	$17	$19
$20	$8	$1	$3	$22

Notes: _____

$300 in 40 Days
Savings Challenge

$5	$6	$9	$15	$13
$23	$12	$7	$2	$24
$16	$14	Free	$10	$4
$11	$18	$21	$17	$19
$20	$8	$1	$3	$22

Notes: _____

$300 in 40 Days
Savings Challenge

$5	$6	$9	$15	$13
$23	$12	$7	$2	$24
$16	$14	Free	$10	$4
$11	$18	$21	$17	$19
$20	$8	$1	$3	$22

Notes:

$300 in 40 Days
Savings Challenge

$5	$6	$9	$15	$13
$23	$12	$7	$2	$24
$16	$14	Free	$10	$4
$11	$18	$21	$17	$19
$20	$8	$1	$3	$22

Notes: _____

$300 in 40 Days

Savings Challenge

$5	$6	$9	$15	$13
$23	$12	$7	$2	$24
$16	$14	Free	$10	$4
$11	$18	$21	$17	$19
$20	$8	$1	$3	$22

Notes: _____

$300 in 40 Days

Savings Challenge

$5	$6	$9	$15	$13
$23	$12	$7	$2	$24
$16	$14	Free	$10	$4
$11	$18	$21	$17	$19
$20	$8	$1	$3	$22

Notes: _____

$300 in 40 Days

Savings Challenge

$5	$6	$9	$15	$13
$23	$12	$7	$2	$24
$16	$14	Free	$10	$4
$11	$18	$21	$17	$19
$20	$8	$1	$3	$22

Notes:

$300 in 40 Days

Savings Challenge

$5	$6	$9	$15	$13
$23	$12	$7	$2	$24
$16	$14	Free	$10	$4
$11	$18	$21	$17	$19
$20	$8	$1	$3	$22

Notes:

$300 in 40 Days

Savings Challenge

$5	$6	$9	$15	$13
$23	$12	$7	$2	$24
$16	$14	Free	$10	$4
$11	$18	$21	$17	$19
$20	$8	$1	$3	$22

Notes: _____

$300 in 40 Days

Savings Challenge

$5	$6	$9	$15	$13
$23	$12	$7	$2	$24
$16	$14	Free	$10	$4
$11	$18	$21	$17	$19
$20	$8	$1	$3	$22

Notes:

$300 in 40 Days

Savings Challenge

$5	$6	$9	$15	$13
$23	$12	$7	$2	$24
$16	$14	Free	$10	$4
$11	$18	$21	$17	$19
$20	$8	$1	$3	$22

Notes:

$300 in 40 Days

Savings Challenge

$5	$6	$9	$15	$13
$23	$12	$7	$2	$24
$16	$14	Free	$10	$4
$11	$18	$21	$17	$19
$20	$8	$1	$3	$22

Notes:

$300 in 40 Days

Savings Challenge

$5	$6	$9	$15	$13
$23	$12	$7	$2	$24
$16	$14	Free	$10	$4
$11	$18	$21	$17	$19
$20	$8	$1	$3	$22

Notes: _____

$300 in 40 Days

Savings Challenge

$5	$6	$9	$15	$13
$23	$12	$7	$2	$24
$16	$14	Free	$10	$4
$11	$18	$21	$17	$19
$20	$8	$1	$3	$22

Notes:

$300 in 40 Days Savings Challenge

$5	$6	$9	$15	$13
$23	$12	$7	$2	$24
$16	$14	Free	$10	$4
$11	$18	$21	$17	$19
$20	$8	$1	$3	$22

Notes:

$100 in 30 Days
Savings Challenge

$1	$4	$6	$9
$10	$5	$8	$7
$7	$10	$9	$5
$4	$8	$6	$1

Notes:

$100 in 30 Days Savings Challenge

$1	$4	$6	$9
$10	$5	$8	$7
$7	$10	$9	$5
$4	$8	$6	$1

Notes: _____

$100 in 30 Days
Savings Challenge

$1	$4	$6	$9
$10	$5	$8	$7
$7	$10	$9	$5
$4	$8	$6	$1

Notes:

$100 in 30 Days
Savings Challenge

$1	$4	$6	$9
$10	$5	$8	$7
$7	$10	$9	$5
$4	$8	$6	$1

Notes:

$100 in 30 Days
Savings Challenge

$1	$4	$6	$9
$10	$5	$8	$7
$7	$10	$9	$5
$4	$8	$6	$1

Notes:

$100 in 30 Days
Savings Challenge

$1	$4	$6	$9
$10	$5	$8	$7
$7	$10	$9	$5
$4	$8	$6	$1

Notes:

$100 in 30 Days Savings Challenge

$1	$4	$6	$9
$10	$5	$8	$7
$7	$10	$9	$5
$4	$8	$6	$1

Notes:

$100 in 30 Days
Savings Challenge

$1	$4	$6	$9
$10	$5	$8	$7
$7	$10	$9	$5
$4	$8	$6	$1

Notes:

$100 in 30 Days Savings Challenge

$1	$4	$6	$9
$10	$5	$8	$7
$7	$10	$9	$5
$4	$8	$6	$1

Notes:

$100 in 30 Days
Savings Challenge

$1	$4	$6	$9
$10	$5	$8	$7
$7	$10	$9	$5
$4	$8	$6	$1

Notes:

$100 in 30 Days
Savings Challenge

$1	$4	$6	$9
$10	$5	$8	$7
$7	$10	$9	$5
$4	$8	$6	$1

Notes:

$100 in 30 Days
Savings Challenge

$1	$4	$6	$9
$10	$5	$8	$7
$7	$10	$9	$5
$4	$8	$6	$1

Notes:

$100 in 30 Days
Savings Challenge

$1	$4	$6	$9
$10	$5	$8	$7
$7	$10	$9	$5
$4	$8	$6	$1

Notes:

$100 in 30 Days Savings Challenge

$1	$4	$6	$9
$10	$5	$8	$7
$7	$10	$9	$5
$4	$8	$6	$1

Notes:

$100 in 30 Days
Savings Challenge

$1	$4	$6	$9
$10	$5	$8	$7
$7	$10	$9	$5
$4	$8	$6	$1

Notes:

$1000 in 12 Weeks
Savings Challenge

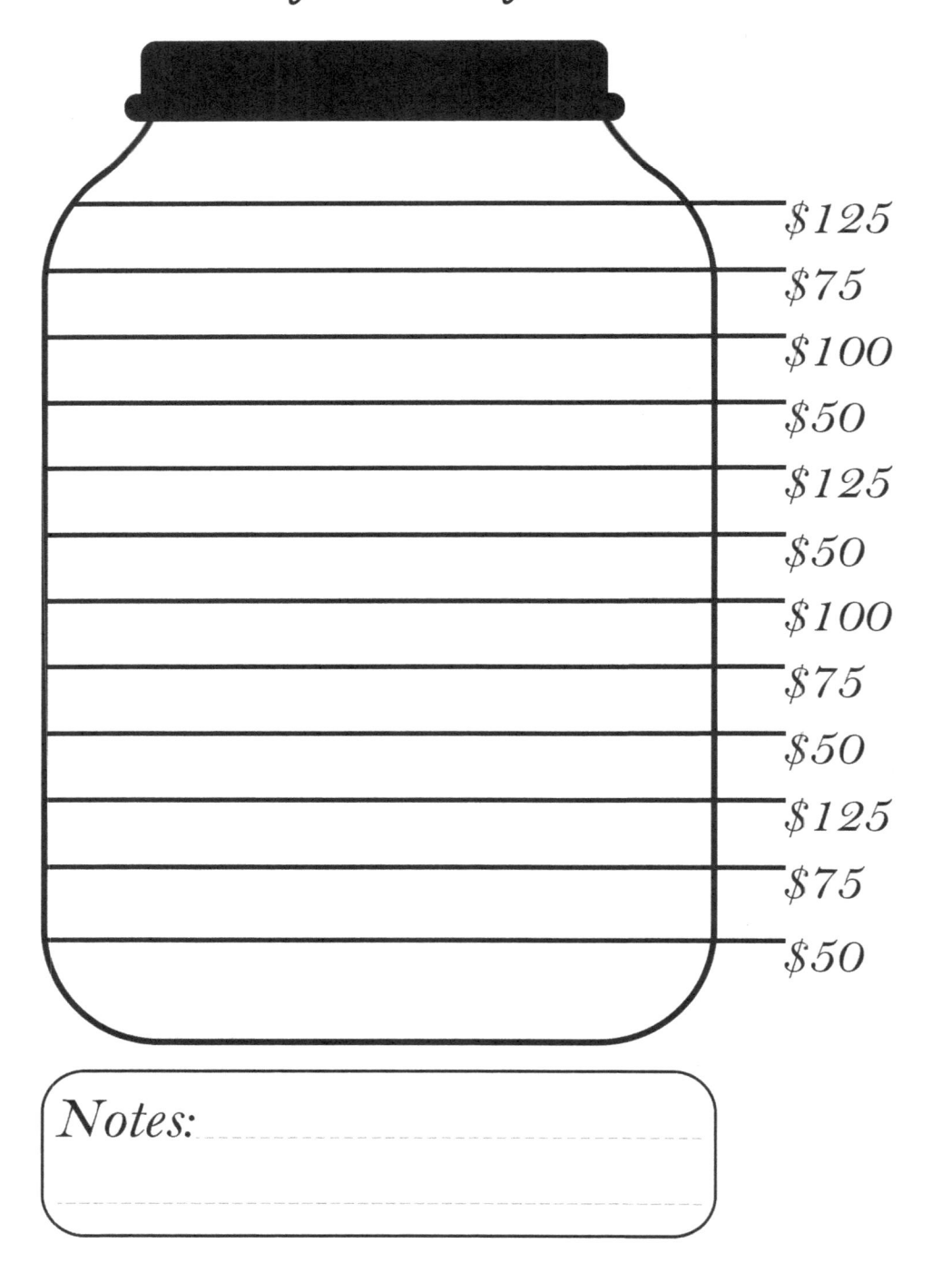

- $125
- $75
- $100
- $50
- $125
- $50
- $100
- $75
- $50
- $125
- $75
- $50

Notes:

$1000 in 12 Weeks
Savings Challenge

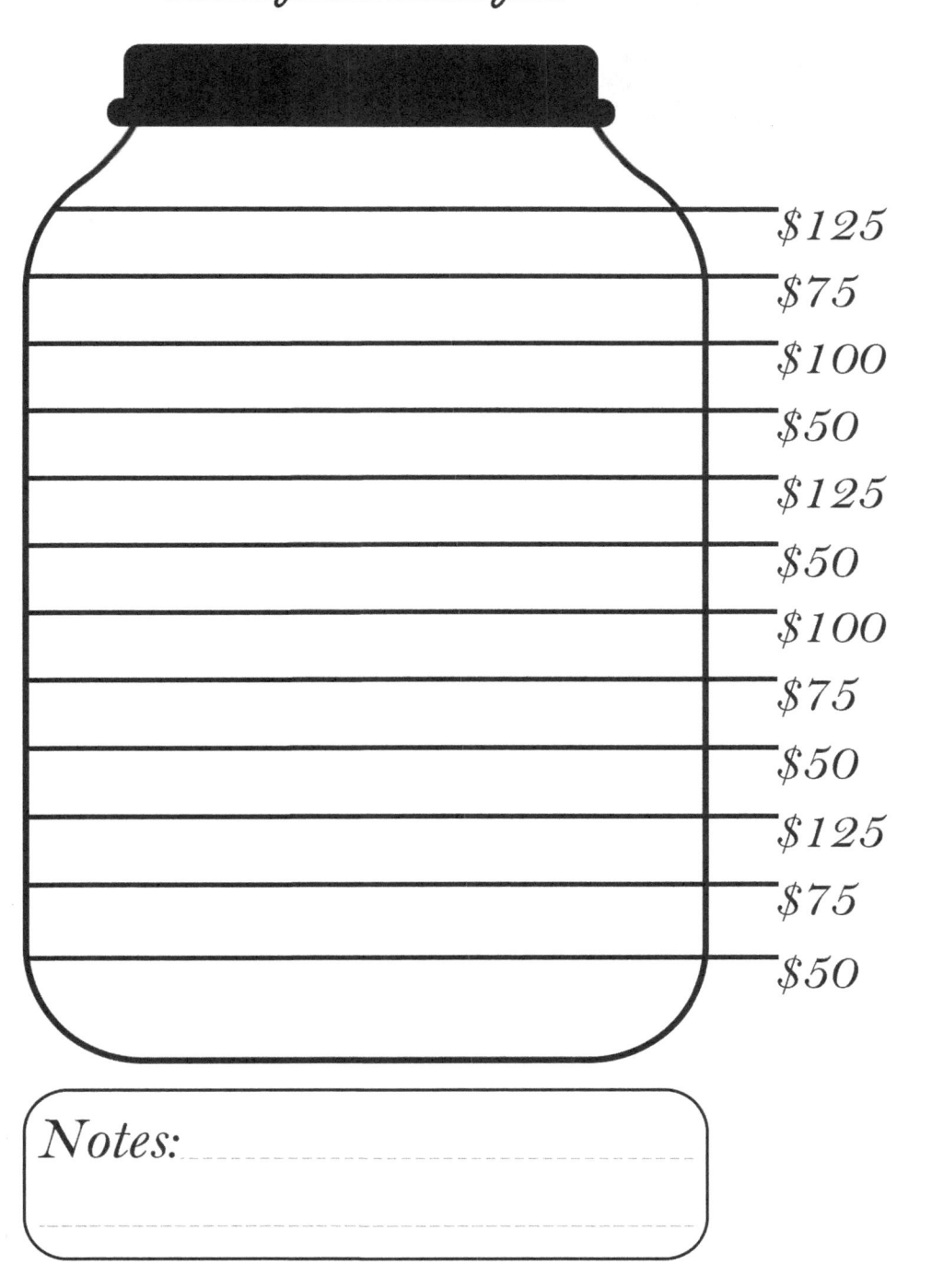

- $125
- $75
- $100
- $50
- $125
- $50
- $100
- $75
- $50
- $125
- $75
- $50

Notes:

$1000 in 12 Weeks
Savings Challenge

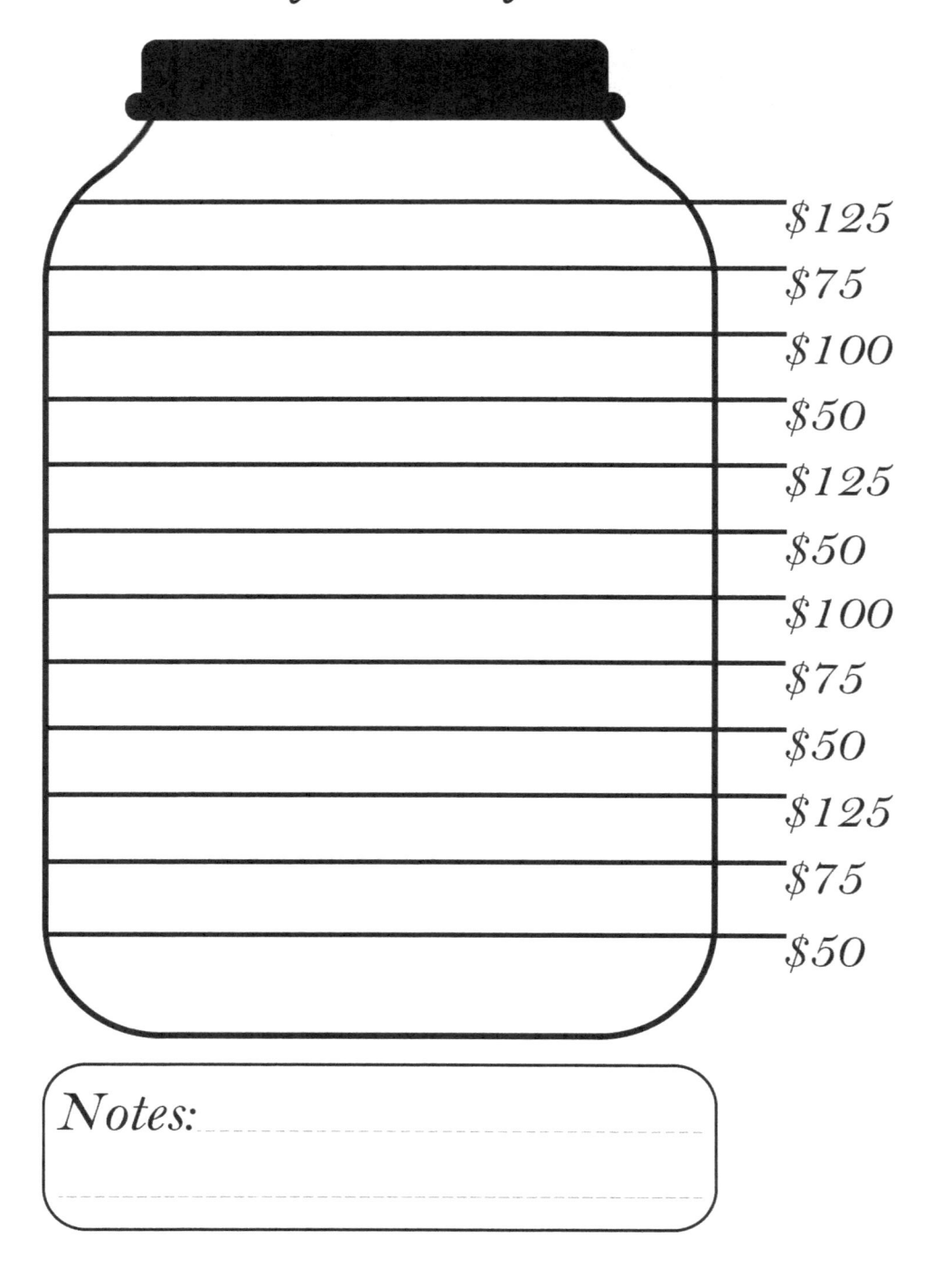

- $125
- $75
- $100
- $50
- $125
- $50
- $100
- $75
- $50
- $125
- $75
- $50

Notes:

$1000 in 12 Weeks
Savings Challenge

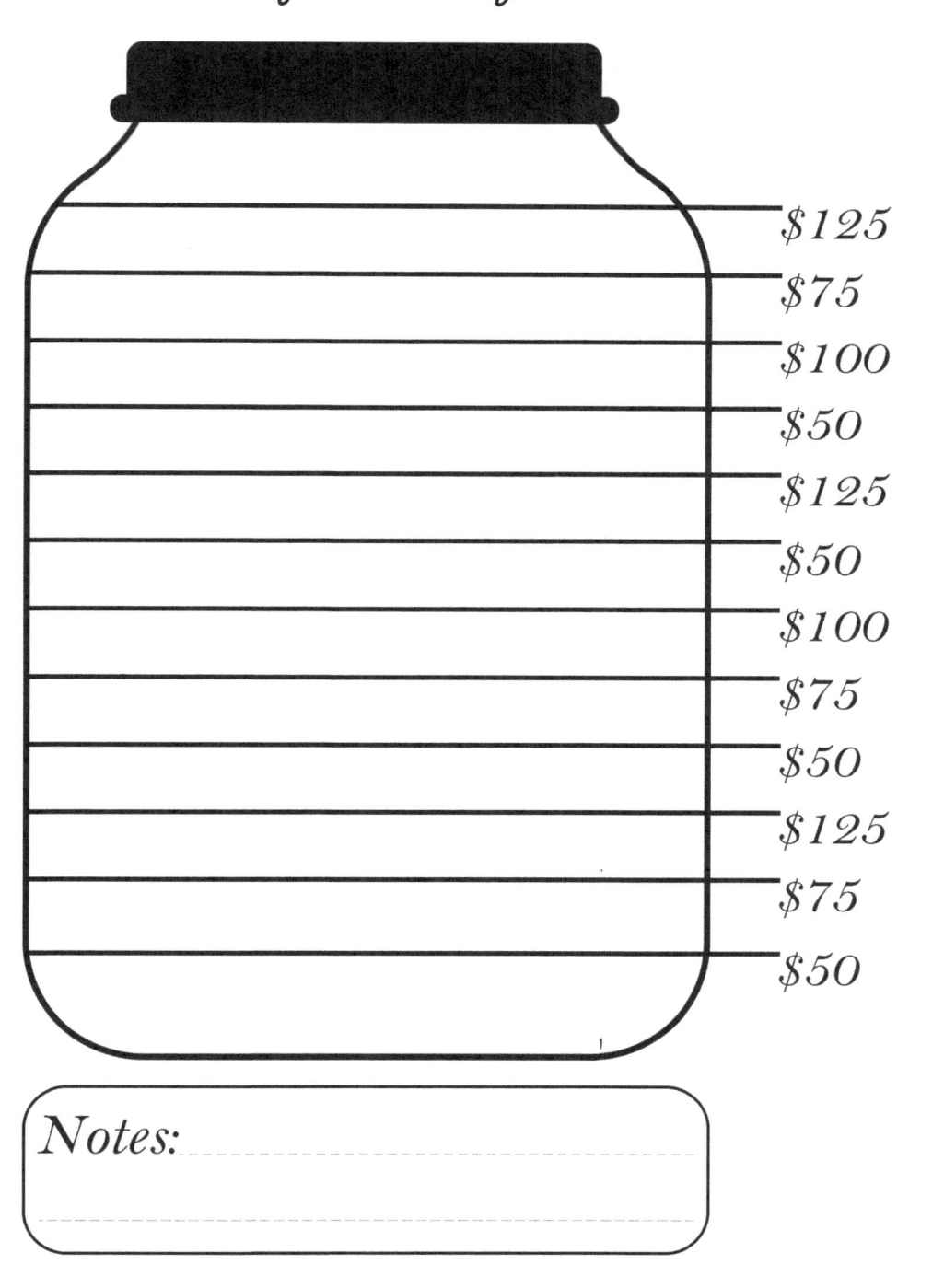

- $125
- $75
- $100
- $50
- $125
- $50
- $100
- $75
- $50
- $125
- $75
- $50

Notes:

$1000 in 12 Weeks Savings Challenge

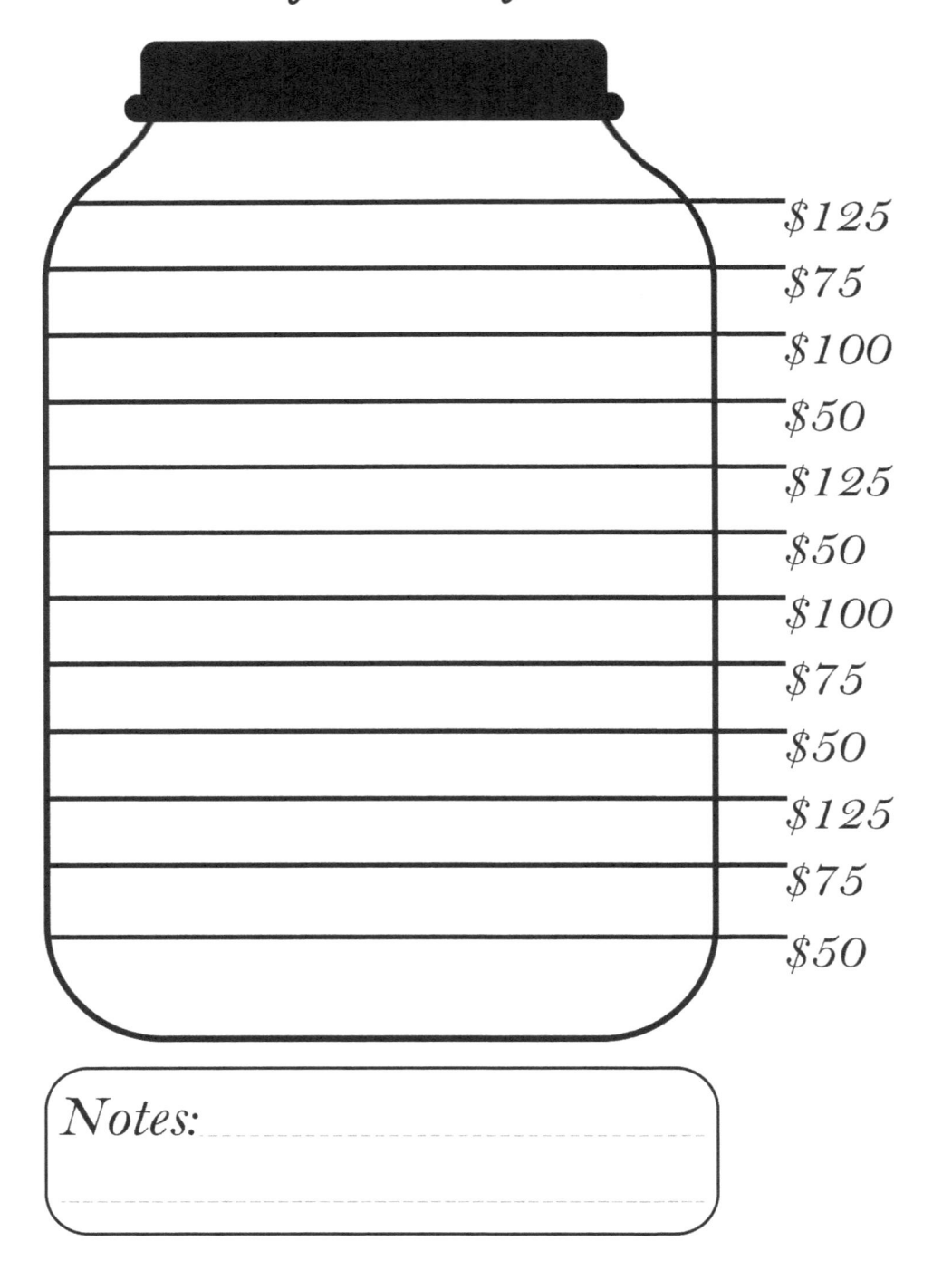

- $125
- $75
- $100
- $50
- $125
- $50
- $100
- $75
- $50
- $125
- $75
- $50

Notes:

$1000 in 12 Weeks
Savings Challenge

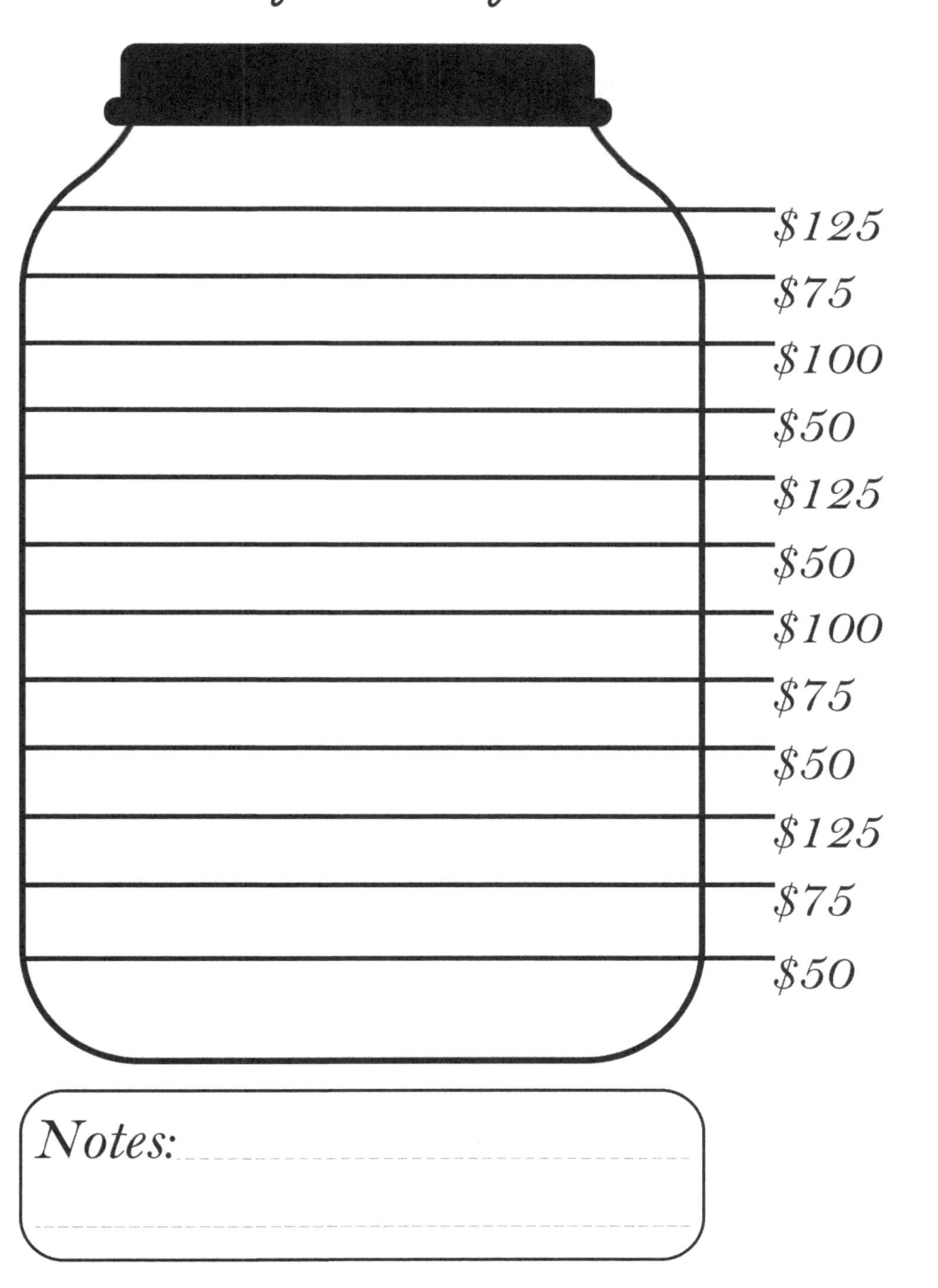

- $125
- $75
- $100
- $50
- $125
- $50
- $100
- $75
- $50
- $125
- $75
- $50

Notes:

$1000 in 12 Weeks Savings Challenge

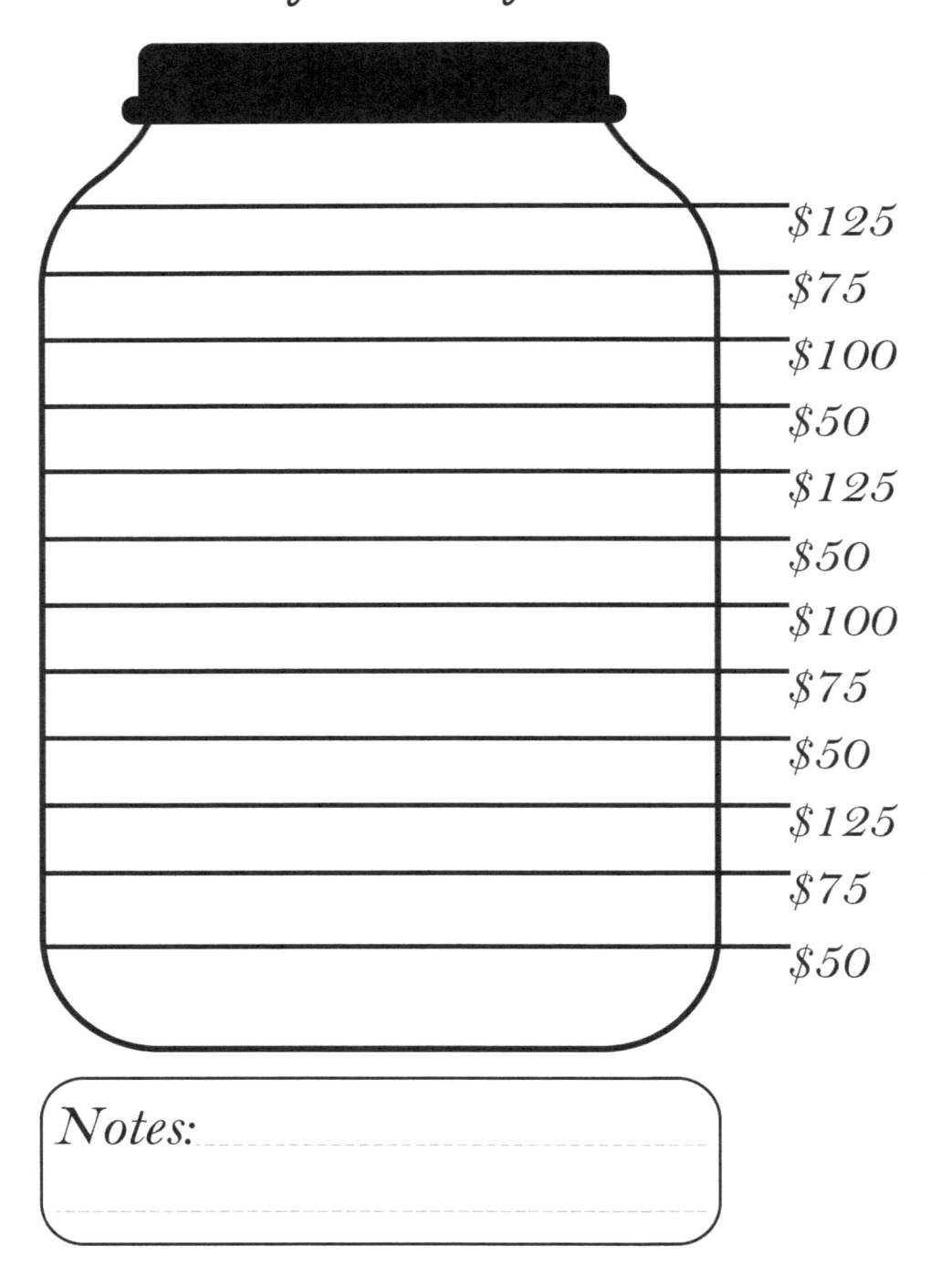

- $125
- $75
- $100
- $50
- $125
- $50
- $100
- $75
- $50
- $125
- $75
- $50

Notes:

$1000 in 12 Weeks
Savings Challenge

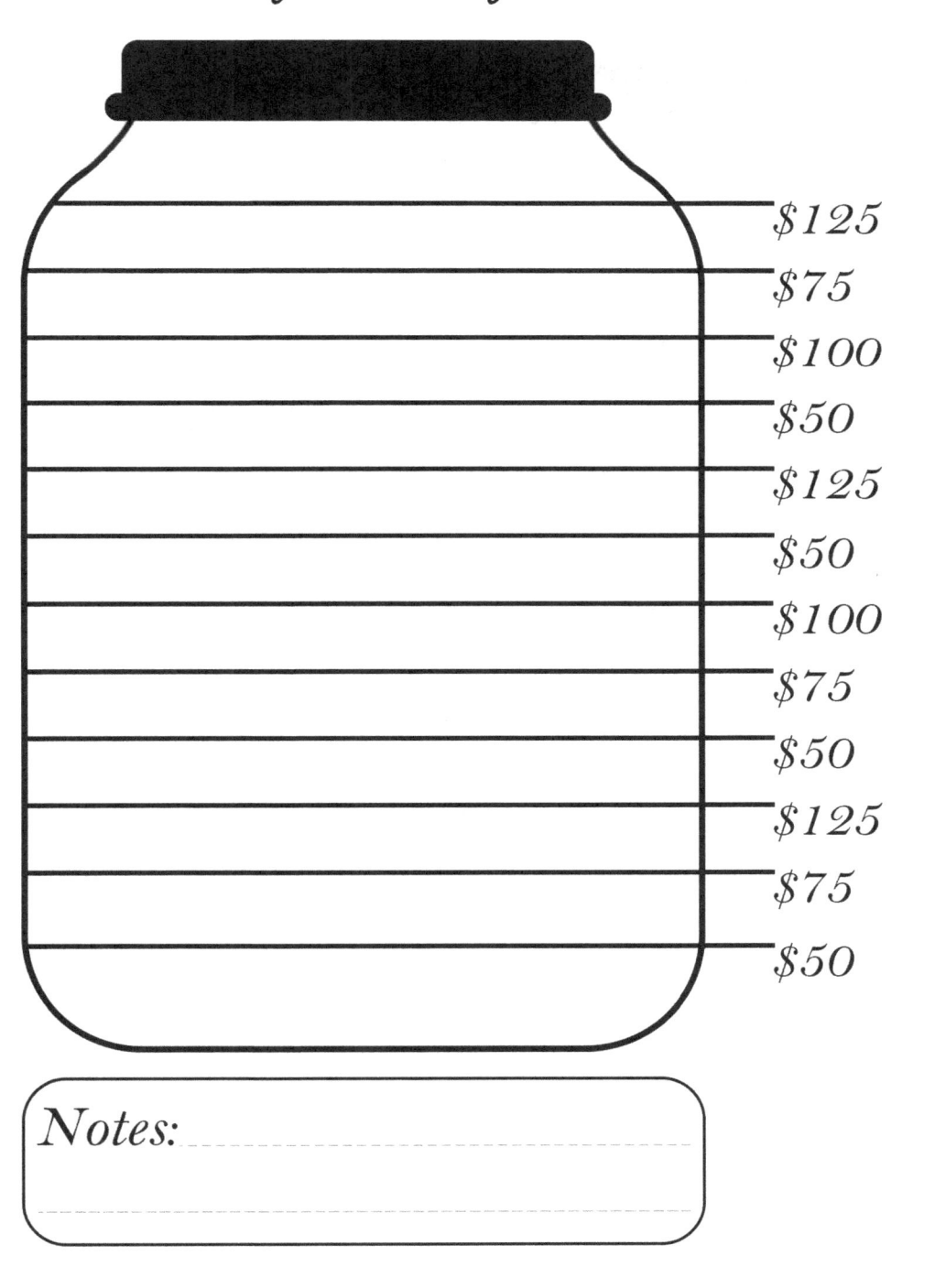

- $125
- $75
- $100
- $50
- $125
- $50
- $100
- $75
- $50
- $125
- $75
- $50

Notes:

$1000 in 12 Weeks Savings Challenge

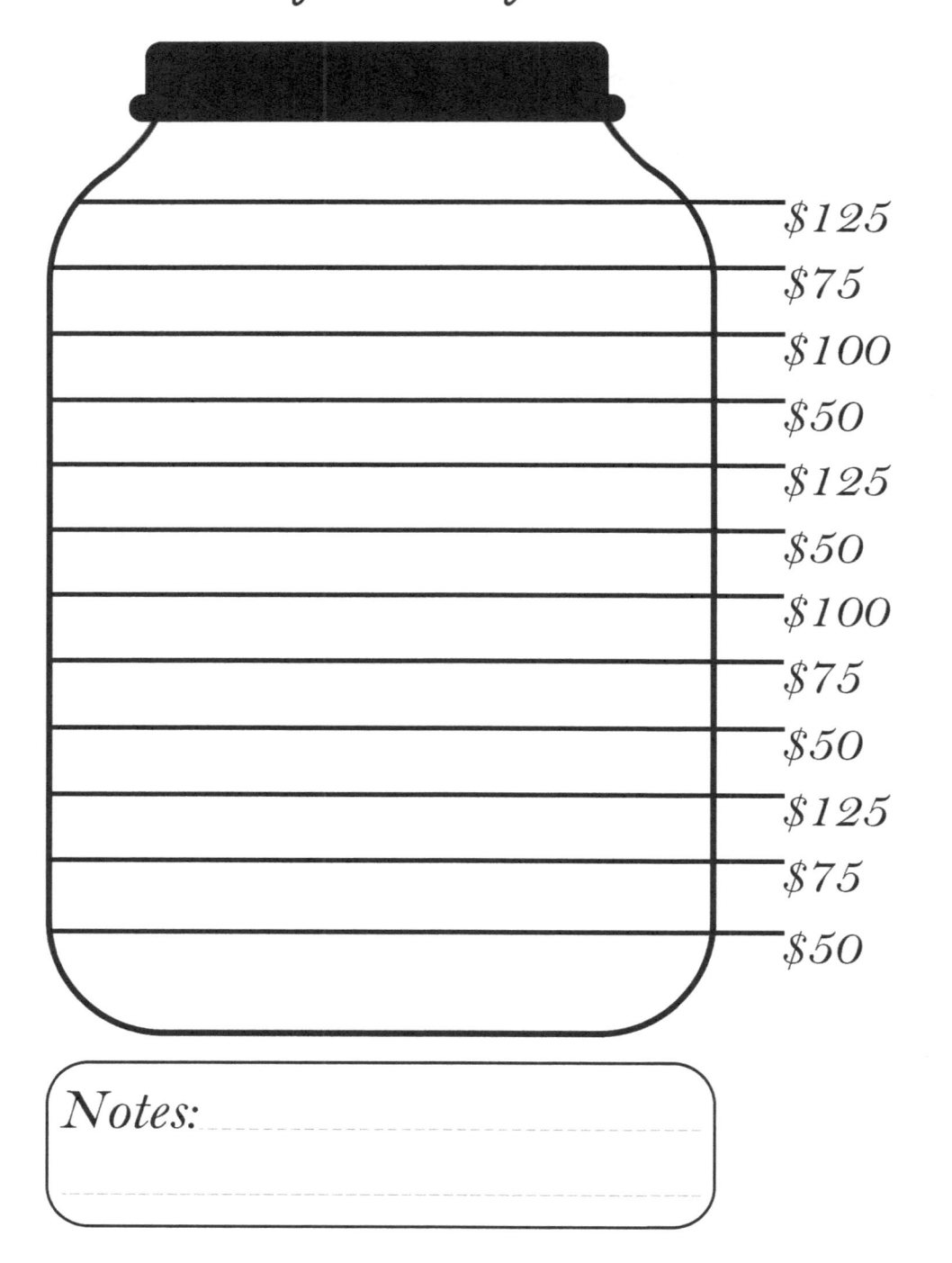

- $125
- $75
- $100
- $50
- $125
- $50
- $100
- $75
- $50
- $125
- $75
- $50

Notes:

$1000 in 12 Weeks
Savings Challenge

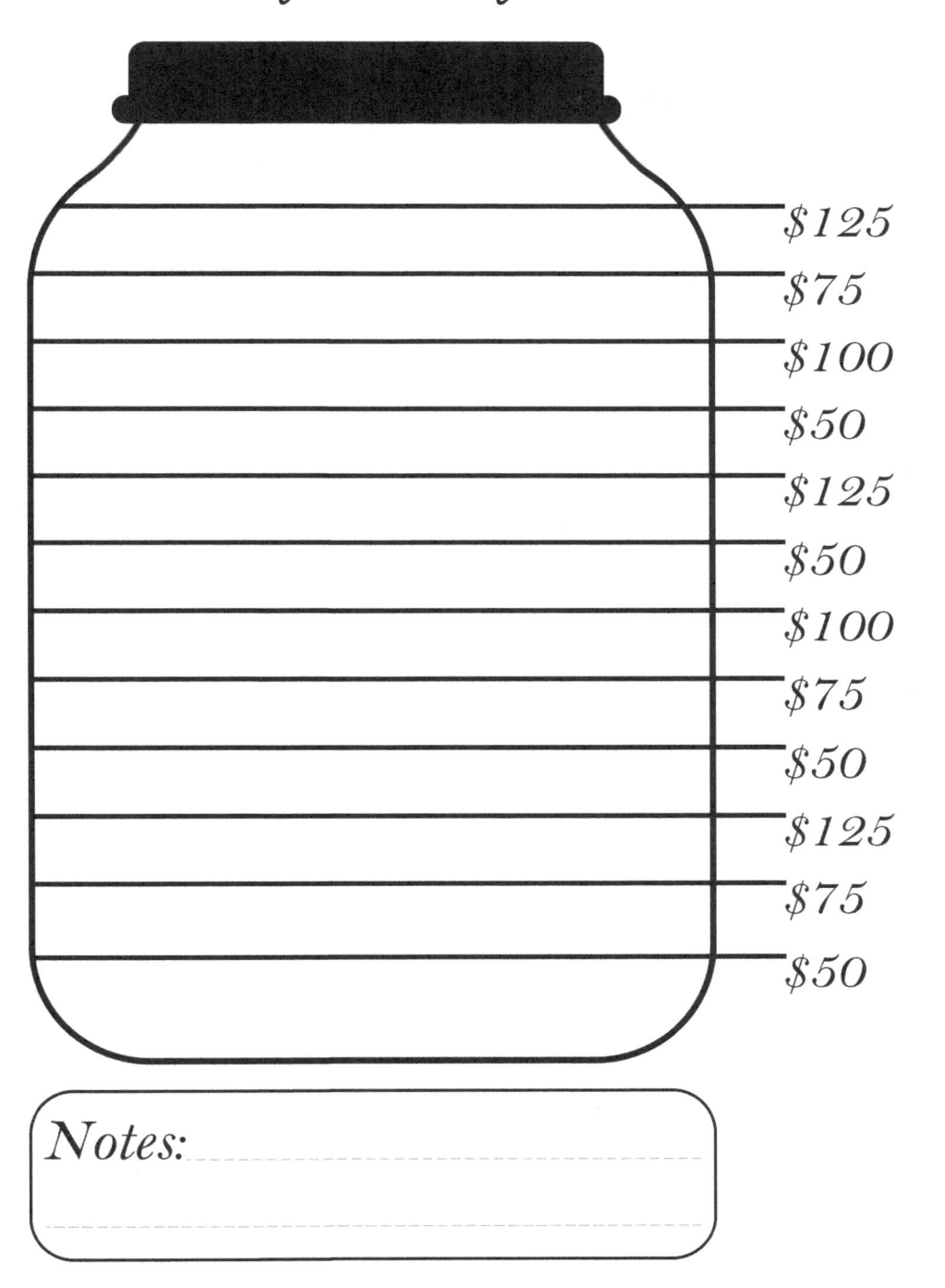

- $125
- $75
- $100
- $50
- $125
- $50
- $100
- $75
- $50
- $125
- $75
- $50

Notes:

$1000 in 12 Weeks Savings Challenge

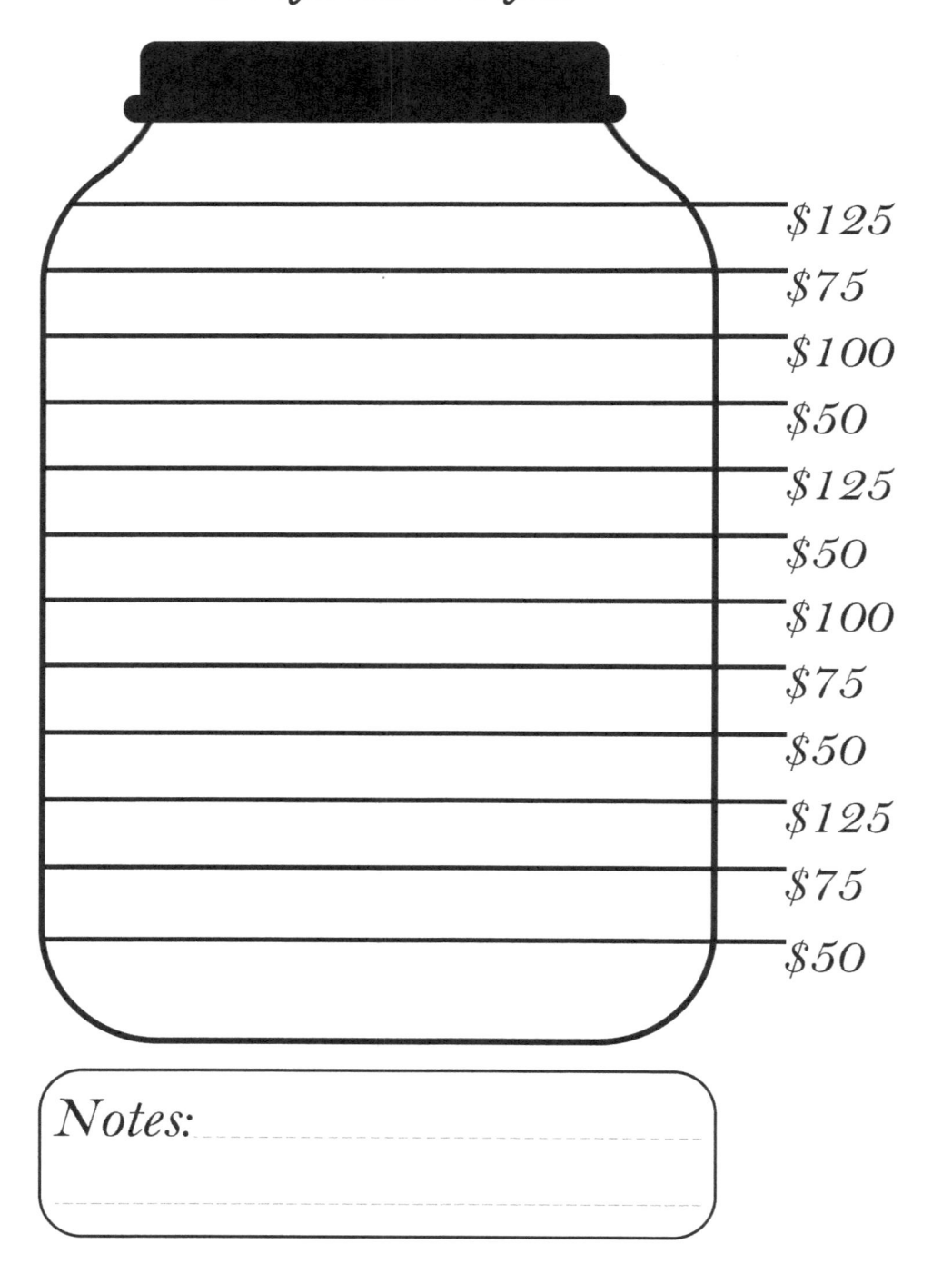

- $125
- $75
- $100
- $50
- $125
- $50
- $100
- $75
- $50
- $125
- $75
- $50

Notes:

$1000 in 12 Weeks
Savings Challenge

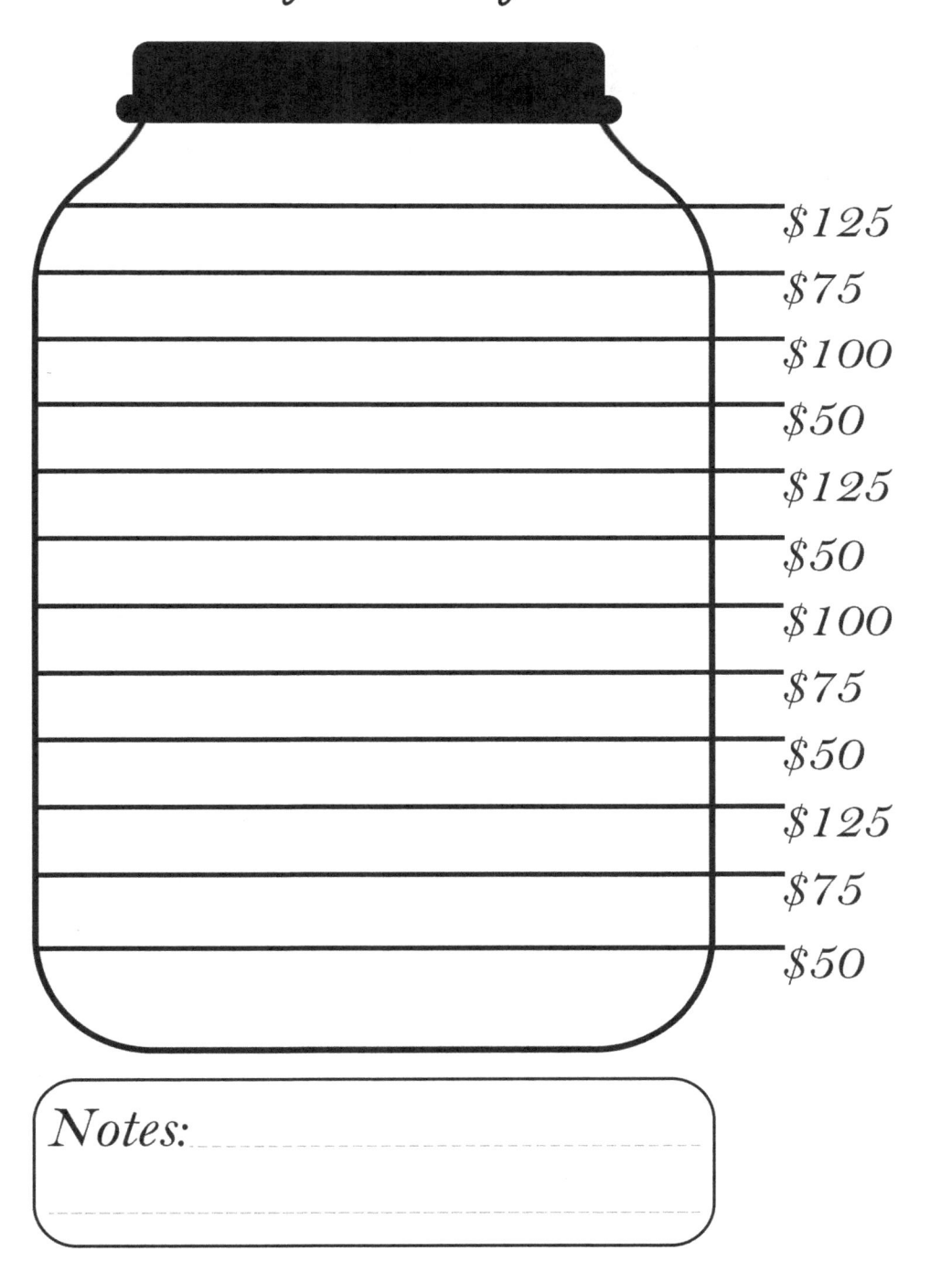

- $125
- $75
- $100
- $50
- $125
- $50
- $100
- $75
- $50
- $125
- $75
- $50

Notes:

$1000 in 12 Weeks
Savings Challenge

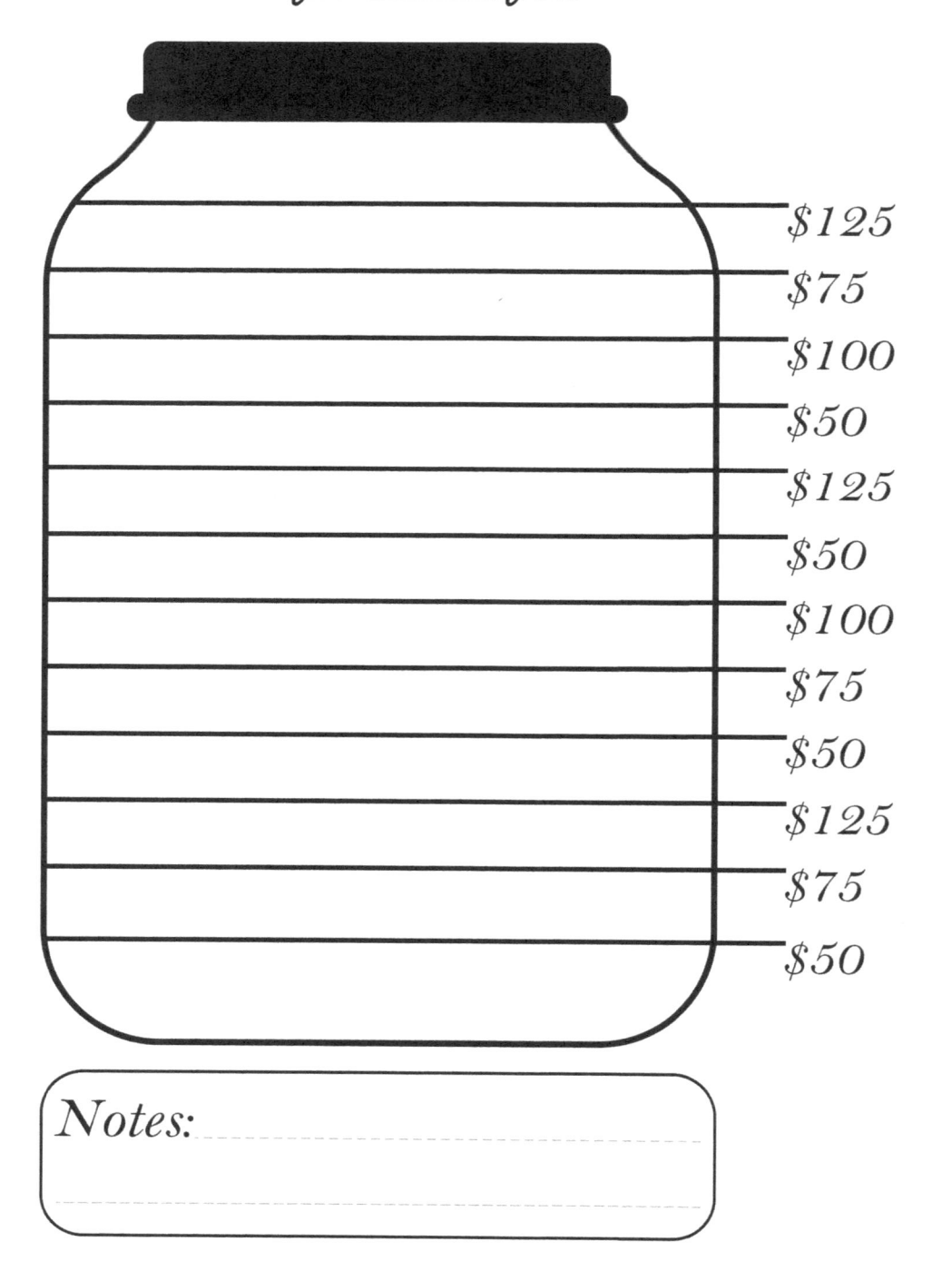

- $125
- $75
- $100
- $50
- $125
- $50
- $100
- $75
- $50
- $125
- $75
- $50

Notes:

$1000 in 12 Weeks Savings Challenge

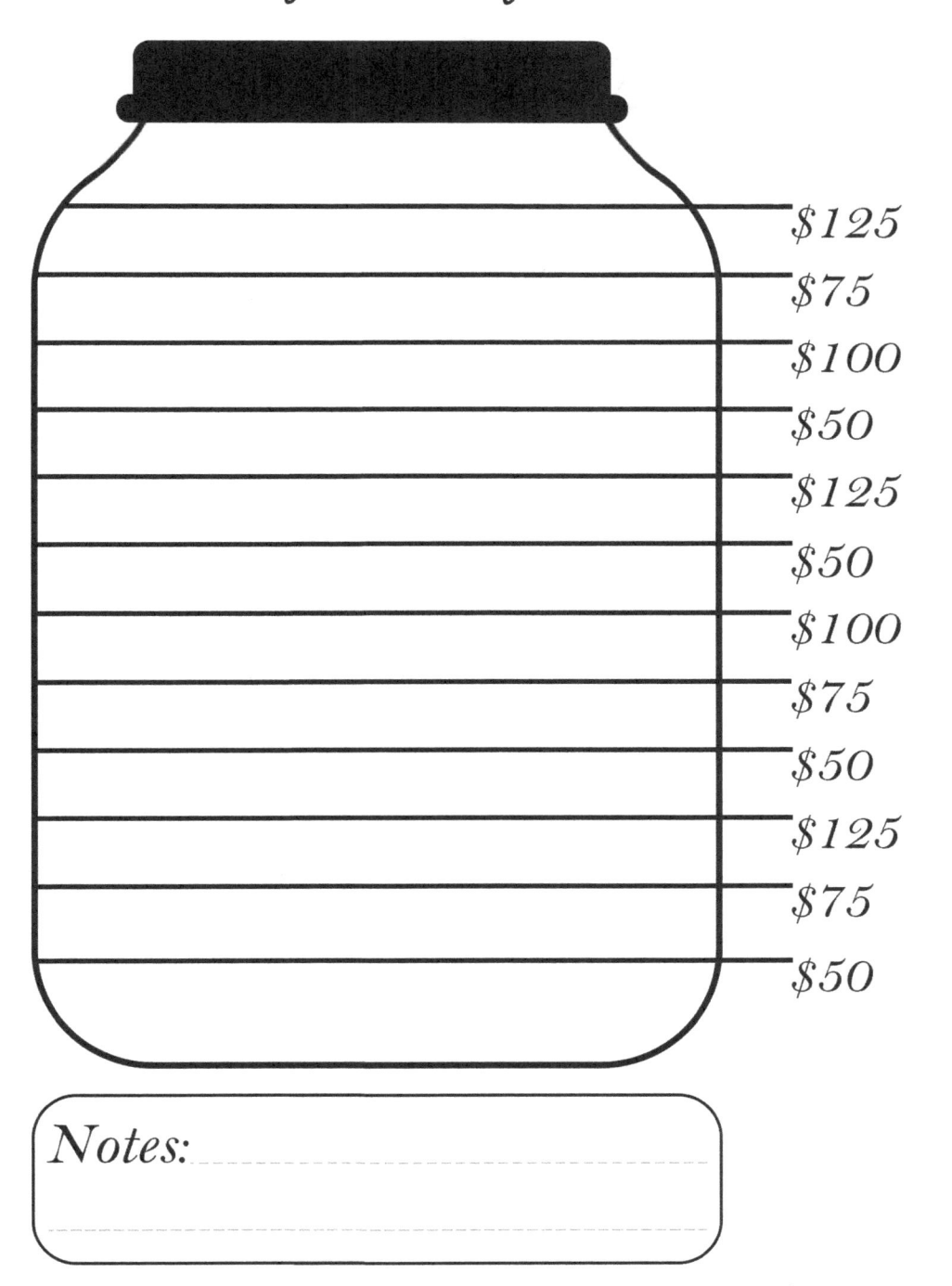

- $125
- $75
- $100
- $50
- $125
- $50
- $100
- $75
- $50
- $125
- $75
- $50

Notes:

$1000 in 12 Weeks Savings Challenge

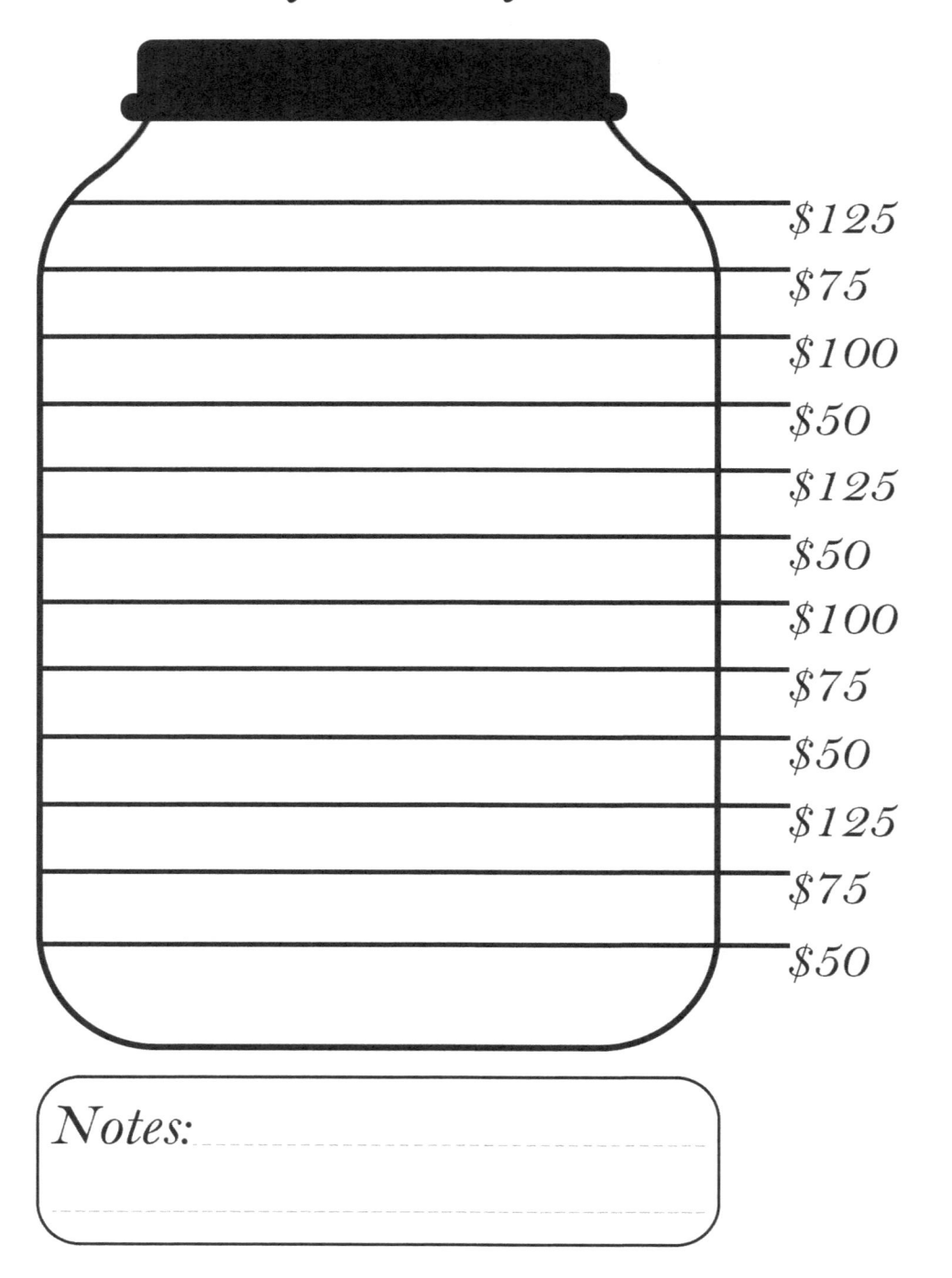

- $125
- $75
- $100
- $50
- $125
- $50
- $100
- $75
- $50
- $125
- $75
- $50

Notes:

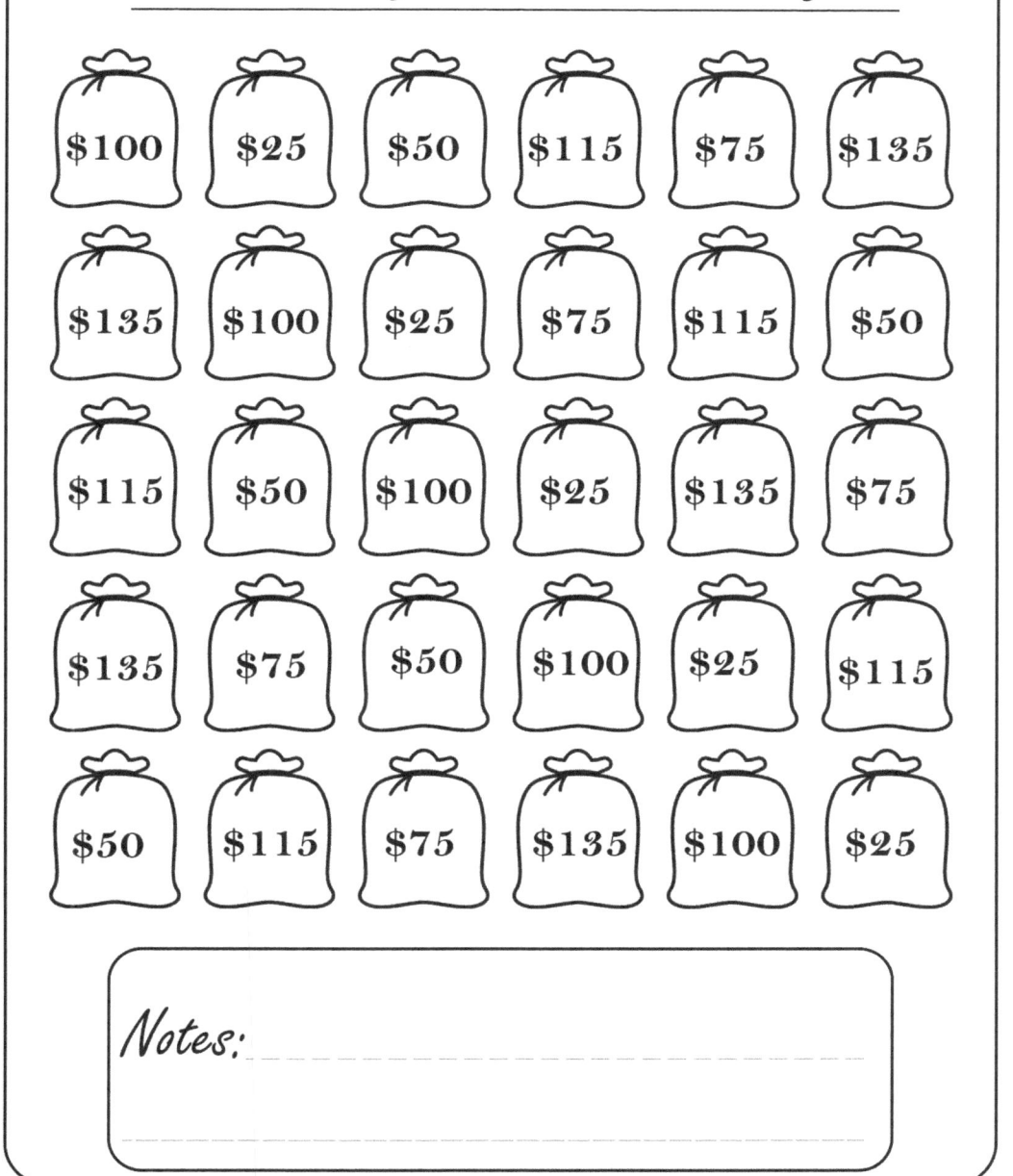

$2500 in 6 Weeks
Savings Challenge

$100	$25	$50	$115	$75	$135
$135	$100	$25	$75	$115	$50
$115	$50	$100	$25	$135	$75
$135	$75	$50	$100	$25	$115
$50	$115	$75	$135	$100	$25

Notes:

$2500 in 6 Weeks
Savings Challenge

$100	$25	$50	$115	$75	$135
$135	$100	$25	$75	$115	$50
$115	$50	$100	$25	$135	$75
$135	$75	$50	$100	$25	$115
$50	$115	$75	$135	$100	$25

Notes: _____

$2500 in 6 Weeks
Savings Challenge

$100	$25	$50	$115	$75	$135
$135	$100	$25	$75	$115	$50
$115	$50	$100	$25	$135	$75
$135	$75	$50	$100	$25	$115
$50	$115	$75	$135	$100	$25

Notes:

$2500 in 6 Weeks
Savings Challenge

$100	$25	$50	$115	$75	$135
$135	$100	$25	$75	$115	$50
$115	$50	$100	$25	$135	$75
$135	$75	$50	$100	$25	$115
$50	$115	$75	$135	$100	$25

Notes: _____

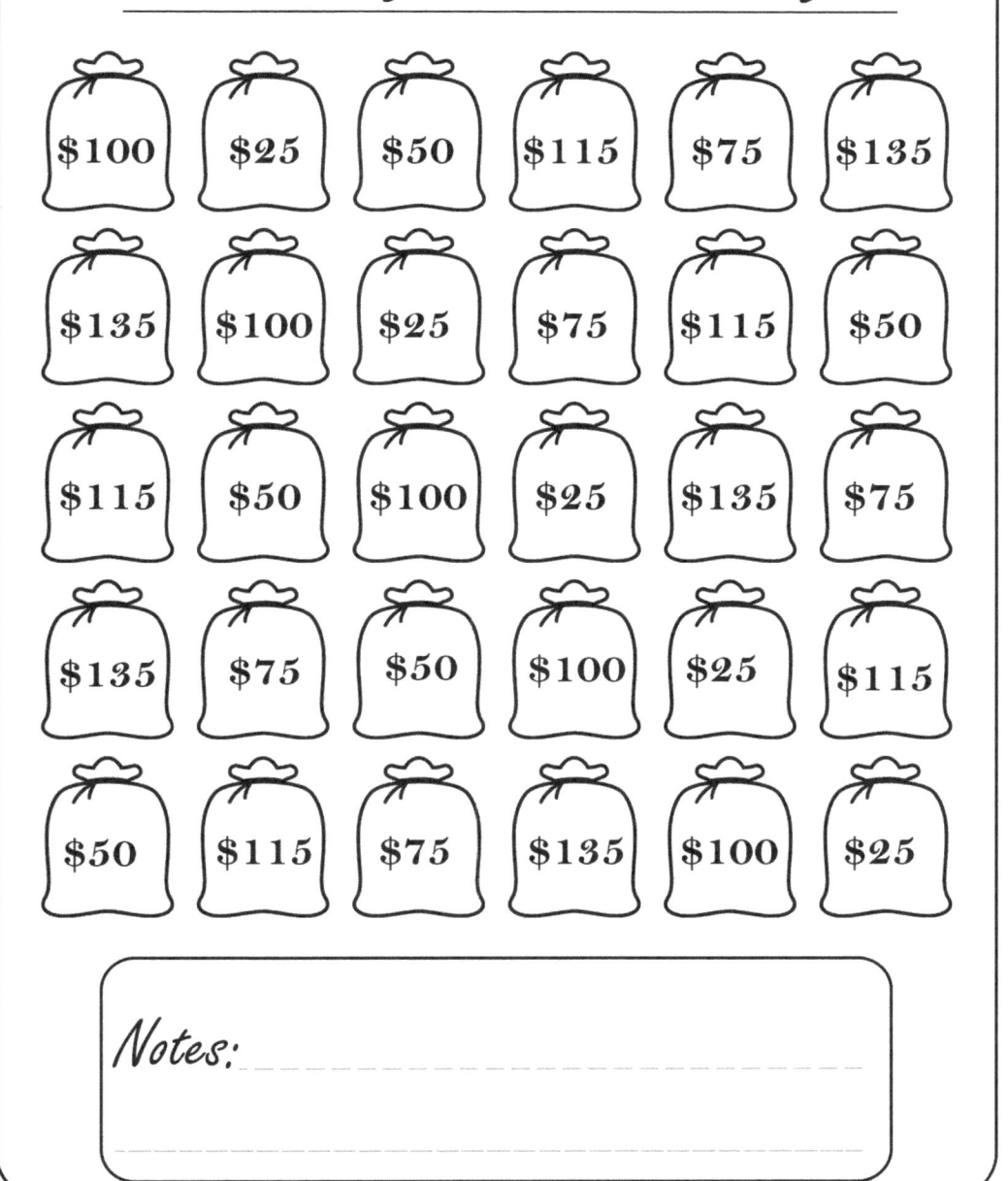

$2500 in 6 Weeks
Savings Challenge

$100	$25	$50	$115	$75	$135
$135	$100	$25	$75	$115	$50
$115	$50	$100	$25	$135	$75
$135	$75	$50	$100	$25	$115
$50	$115	$75	$135	$100	$25

Notes: _____

$2500 in 6 Weeks
Savings Challenge

$100	$25	$50	$115	$75	$135
$135	$100	$25	$75	$115	$50
$115	$50	$100	$25	$135	$75
$135	$75	$50	$100	$25	$115
$50	$115	$75	$135	$100	$25

Notes: _____

$2500 in 6 Weeks
Savings Challenge

$100	$25	$50	$115	$75	$135
$135	$100	$25	$75	$115	$50
$115	$50	$100	$25	$135	$75
$135	$75	$50	$100	$25	$115
$50	$115	$75	$135	$100	$25

Notes:

$2500 in 6 Weeks
Savings Challenge

$100	$25	$50	$115	$75	$135
$135	$100	$25	$75	$115	$50
$115	$50	$100	$25	$135	$75
$135	$75	$50	$100	$25	$115
$50	$115	$75	$135	$100	$25

Notes:

$2500 in 6 Weeks
Savings Challenge

$100	$25	$50	$115	$75	$135
$135	$100	$25	$75	$115	$50
$115	$50	$100	$25	$135	$75
$135	$75	$50	$100	$25	$115
$50	$115	$75	$135	$100	$25

Notes:

$2500 in 6 Weeks
Savings Challenge

$100	$25	$50	$115	$75	$135
$135	$100	$25	$75	$115	$50
$115	$50	$100	$25	$135	$75
$135	$75	$50	$100	$25	$115
$50	$115	$75	$135	$100	$25

Notes: _____

$2500 in 6 Weeks

Savings Challenge

$100	$25	$50	$115	$75	$135
$135	$100	$25	$75	$115	$50
$115	$50	$100	$25	$135	$75
$135	$75	$50	$100	$25	$115
$50	$115	$75	$135	$100	$25

Notes: _____

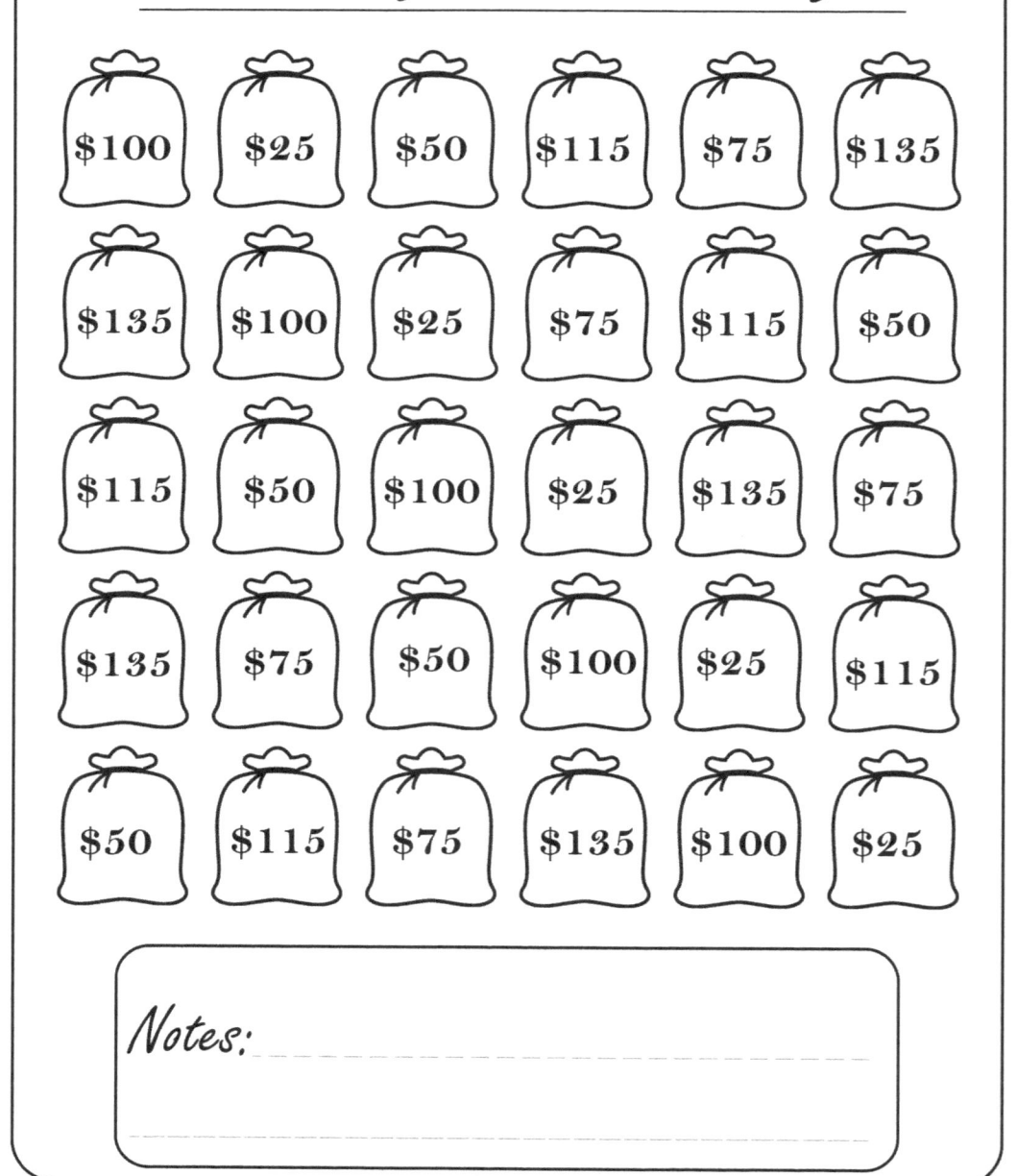

$2500 in 6 Weeks

Savings Challenge

$100	$25	$50	$115	$75	$135
$135	$100	$25	$75	$115	$50
$115	$50	$100	$25	$135	$75
$135	$75	$50	$100	$25	$115
$50	$115	$75	$135	$100	$25

Notes:

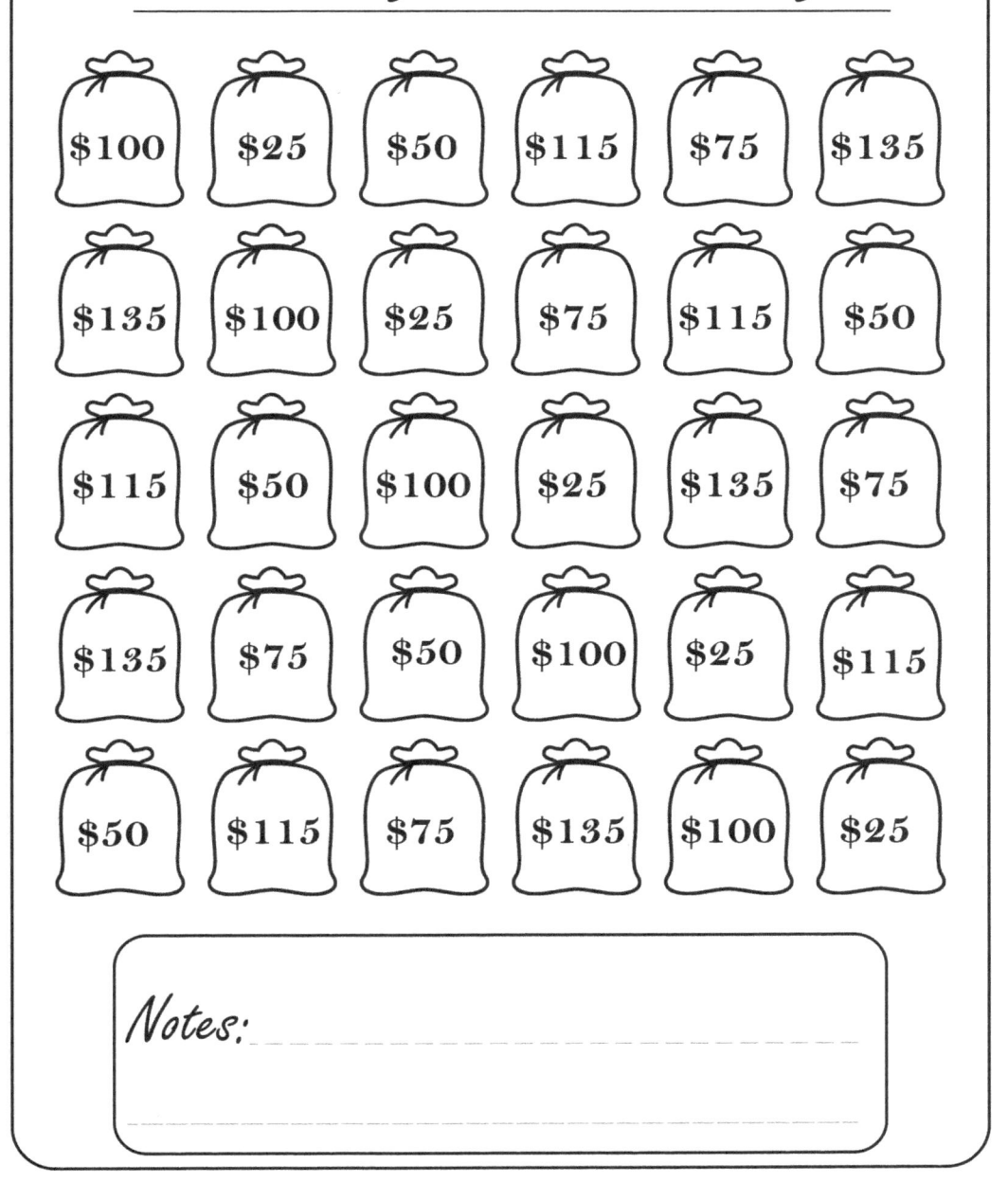

$2500 in 6 Weeks
Savings Challenge

$100	$25	$50	$115	$75	$135
$135	$100	$25	$75	$115	$50
$115	$50	$100	$25	$135	$75
$135	$75	$50	$100	$25	$115
$50	$115	$75	$135	$100	$25

Notes:

$2500 in 6 Weeks
Savings Challenge

$100	$25	$50	$115	$75	$135
$135	$100	$25	$75	$115	$50
$115	$50	$100	$25	$135	$75
$135	$75	$50	$100	$25	$115
$50	$115	$75	$135	$100	$25

Notes:

$2500 in 6 Weeks
Savings Challenge

$100	$25	$50	$115	$75	$135
$135	$100	$25	$75	$115	$50
$115	$50	$100	$25	$135	$75
$135	$75	$50	$100	$25	$115
$50	$115	$75	$135	$100	$25

Notes: _____

$2500 in 1 Year

Savings Challenge

$25	$25	$25	$30	$30	$30
$35	$35	$35	$40	$40	$40
$45	$45	$45	$50	$50	$50
$55	$55	$55	$60	$60	$60
$68	$68	$68	$75	$75	$75
$80	$80	$80	$85	$85	$85
$90	$90	$90	$95	$95	$96

Notes:

$2500 in 1 Year
Savings Challenge

$25	$25	$25	$30	$30	$30
$35	$35	$35	$40	$40	$40
$45	$45	$45	$50	$50	$50
$55	$55	$55	$60	$60	$60
$68	$68	$68	$75	$75	$75
$80	$80	$80	$85	$85	$85
$90	$90	$90	$95	$95	$96

Notes:

$2500 in 1 Year
Savings Challenge

$25	$25	$25	$30	$30	$30
$35	$35	$35	$40	$40	$40
$45	$45	$45	$50	$50	$50
$55	$55	$55	$60	$60	$60
$68	$68	$68	$75	$75	$75
$80	$80	$80	$85	$85	$85
$90	$90	$90	$95	$95	$96

Notes:

$2500 in 1 Year

Savings Challenge

$25	$25	$25	$30	$30	$30
$35	$35	$35	$40	$40	$40
$45	$45	$45	$50	$50	$50
$55	$55	$55	$60	$60	$60
$68	$68	$68	$75	$75	$75
$80	$80	$80	$85	$85	$85
$90	$90	$90	$95	$95	$96

Notes:

$2500 in 1 Year
Savings Challenge

$25	$25	$25	$30	$30	$30
$35	$35	$35	$40	$40	$40
$45	$45	$45	$50	$50	$50
$55	$55	$55	$60	$60	$60
$68	$68	$68	$75	$75	$75
$80	$80	$80	$85	$85	$85
$90	$90	$90	$95	$95	$96

Notes:

$2500 in 1 Year
Savings Challenge

$25	$25	$25	$30	$30	$30
$35	$35	$35	$40	$40	$40
$45	$45	$45	$50	$50	$50
$55	$55	$55	$60	$60	$60
$68	$68	$68	$75	$75	$75
$80	$80	$80	$85	$85	$85
$90	$90	$90	$95	$95	$96

Notes:

$2500 in 1 Year
Savings Challenge

$25	$25	$25	$30	$30	$30
$35	$35	$35	$40	$40	$40
$45	$45	$45	$50	$50	$50
$55	$55	$55	$60	$60	$60
$68	$68	$68	$75	$75	$75
$80	$80	$80	$85	$85	$85
$90	$90	$90	$95	$95	$96

Notes:

$2500 in 1 Year

Savings Challenge

$25	$25	$25	$30	$30	$30
$35	$35	$35	$40	$40	$40
$45	$45	$45	$50	$50	$50
$55	$55	$55	$60	$60	$60
$68	$68	$68	$75	$75	$75
$80	$80	$80	$85	$85	$85
$90	$90	$90	$95	$95	$96

Notes:

$2500 in 1 Year
Savings Challenge

$25	$25	$25	$30	$30	$30
$35	$35	$35	$40	$40	$40
$45	$45	$45	$50	$50	$50
$55	$55	$55	$60	$60	$60
$68	$68	$68	$75	$75	$75
$80	$80	$80	$85	$85	$85
$90	$90	$90	$95	$95	$96

Notes:

$2500 in 1 Year

Savings Challenge

$25	$25	$25	$30	$30	$30
$35	$35	$35	$40	$40	$40
$45	$45	$45	$50	$50	$50
$55	$55	$55	$60	$60	$60
$68	$68	$68	$75	$75	$75
$80	$80	$80	$85	$85	$85
$90	$90	$90	$95	$95	$96

Notes:

$2500 in 1 Year
Savings Challenge

$25	$25	$25	$30	$30	$30
$35	$35	$35	$40	$40	$40
$45	$45	$45	$50	$50	$50
$55	$55	$55	$60	$60	$60
$68	$68	$68	$75	$75	$75
$80	$80	$80	$85	$85	$85
$90	$90	$90	$95	$95	$96

Notes:

$2500 in 1 Year

Savings Challenge

$25	$25	$25	$30	$30	$30
$35	$35	$35	$40	$40	$40
$45	$45	$45	$50	$50	$50
$55	$55	$55	$60	$60	$60
$68	$68	$68	$75	$75	$75
$80	$80	$80	$85	$85	$85
$90	$90	$90	$95	$95	$96

Notes:

$2500 in 1 Year
Savings Challenge

$25	$25	$25	$30	$30	$30
$35	$35	$35	$40	$40	$40
$45	$45	$45	$50	$50	$50
$55	$55	$55	$60	$60	$60
$68	$68	$68	$75	$75	$75
$80	$80	$80	$85	$85	$85
$90	$90	$90	$95	$95	$96

Notes:

$2500 in 1 Year
Savings Challenge

$25	$25	$25	$30	$30	$30
$35	$35	$35	$40	$40	$40
$45	$45	$45	$50	$50	$50
$55	$55	$55	$60	$60	$60
$68	$68	$68	$75	$75	$75
$80	$80	$80	$85	$85	$85
$90	$90	$90	$95	$95	$96

Notes:

$2500 in 1 Year
Savings Challenge

$25	$25	$25	$30	$30	$30
$35	$35	$35	$40	$40	$40
$45	$45	$45	$50	$50	$50
$55	$55	$55	$60	$60	$60
$68	$68	$68	$75	$75	$75
$80	$80	$80	$85	$85	$85
$90	$90	$90	$95	$95	$96

Notes:

$10,000 in 52 Weeks
Savings Challenge

$100	$100	$100	$100	$100	$100	$100
$100	$100	$100	$100	$100	$150	$150
$150	$150	$150	$150	$150	$150	$150
$150	$150	$150	$150	$150	$200	$200
$200	$200	$200	$200	$200	$200	$250
$250	$250	$250	$250	$250	$250	$250
$250	$300	$300	$300	$300	$300	$300
$350	$350	$350				

Notes:

$10,000 in 52 Weeks Savings Challenge

$100	$100	$100	$100	$100	$100	$100
$100	$100	$100	$100	$100	$150	$150
$150	$150	$150	$150	$150	$150	$150
$150	$150	$150	$150	$150	$200	$200
$200	$200	$200	$200	$200	$200	$250
$250	$250	$250	$250	$250	$250	$250
$250	$300	$300	$300	$300	$300	$300
$350	$350	$350				

Notes:

$10,000 in 52 Weeks Savings Challenge

$100	$100	$100	$100	$100	$100	$100
$100	$100	$100	$100	$100	$150	$150
$150	$150	$150	$150	$150	$150	$150
$150	$150	$150	$150	$150	$200	$200
$200	$200	$200	$200	$200	$200	$250
$250	$250	$250	$250	$250	$250	$250
$250	$300	$300	$300	$300	$300	$300
$350	$350	$350				

Notes:

$10,000 in 52 Weeks
Savings Challenge

$100	$100	$100	$100	$100	$100	$100
$100	$100	$100	$100	$100	$150	$150
$150	$150	$150	$150	$150	$150	$150
$150	$150	$150	$150	$150	$200	$200
$200	$200	$200	$200	$200	$200	$250
$250	$250	$250	$250	$250	$250	$250
$250	$300	$300	$300	$300	$300	$300
$350	$350	$350				

Notes:

$10,000 in 52 Weeks Savings Challenge

$100	$100	$100	$100	$100	$100	$100
$100	$100	$100	$100	$100	$150	$150
$150	$150	$150	$150	$150	$150	$150
$150	$150	$150	$150	$150	$200	$200
$200	$200	$200	$200	$200	$200	$250
$250	$250	$250	$250	$250	$250	$250
$250	$300	$300	$300	$300	$300	$300
$350	$350	$350				

Notes:

$10,000 in 52 Weeks
Savings Challenge

$100	$100	$100	$100	$100	$100	$100
$100	$100	$100	$100	$100	$150	$150
$150	$150	$150	$150	$150	$150	$150
$150	$150	$150	$150	$150	$200	$200
$200	$200	$200	$200	$200	$200	$250
$250	$250	$250	$250	$250	$250	$250
$250	$300	$300	$300	$300	$300	$300
$350	$350	$350				

Notes:

$10,000 in 52 Weeks Savings Challenge

$100	$100	$100	$100	$100	$100	$100
$100	$100	$100	$100	$100	$150	$150
$150	$150	$150	$150	$150	$150	$150
$150	$150	$150	$150	$150	$200	$200
$200	$200	$200	$200	$200	$200	$250
$250	$250	$250	$250	$250	$250	$250
$250	$300	$300	$300	$300	$300	$300
$350	$350	$350				

Notes:

$10,000 in 52 Weeks Savings Challenge

$100	$100	$100	$100	$100	$100	$100
$100	$100	$100	$100	$100	$150	$150
$150	$150	$150	$150	$150	$150	$150
$150	$150	$150	$150	$150	$200	$200
$200	$200	$200	$200	$200	$200	$250
$250	$250	$250	$250	$250	$250	$250
$250	$300	$300	$300	$300	$300	$300
$350	$350	$350				

Notes:

$10,000 in 52 Weeks Savings Challenge

$100	$100	$100	$100	$100	$100	$100
$100	$100	$100	$100	$100	$150	$150
$150	$150	$150	$150	$150	$150	$150
$150	$150	$150	$150	$150	$200	$200
$200	$200	$200	$200	$200	$200	$250
$250	$250	$250	$250	$250	$250	$250
$250	$300	$300	$300	$300	$300	$300
$350	$350	$350				

Notes:

$10,000 in 52 Weeks Savings Challenge

$100	$100	$100	$100	$100	$100	$100
$100	$100	$100	$100	$100	$150	$150
$150	$150	$150	$150	$150	$150	$150
$150	$150	$150	$150	$150	$200	$200
$200	$200	$200	$200	$200	$200	$250
$250	$250	$250	$250	$250	$250	$250
$250	$300	$300	$300	$300	$300	$300
$350	$350	$350				

Notes:

$10,000 in 52 Weeks Savings Challenge

$100	$100	$100	$100	$100	$100	$100
$100	$100	$100	$100	$100	$150	$150
$150	$150	$150	$150	$150	$150	$150
$150	$150	$150	$150	$150	$200	$200
$200	$200	$200	$200	$200	$200	$250
$250	$250	$250	$250	$250	$250	$250
$250	$300	$300	$300	$300	$300	$300
$350	$350	$350				

Notes:

$10,000 in 52 Weeks Savings Challenge

$100	$100	$100	$100	$100	$100	$100
$100	$100	$100	$100	$100	$150	$150
$150	$150	$150	$150	$150	$150	$150
$150	$150	$150	$150	$150	$200	$200
$200	$200	$200	$200	$200	$200	$250
$250	$250	$250	$250	$250	$250	$250
$250	$300	$300	$300	$300	$300	$300
$350	$350	$350				

Notes:

$10,000 in 52 Weeks Savings Challenge

$100	$100	$100	$100	$100	$100	$100
$100	$100	$100	$100	$100	$150	$150
$150	$150	$150	$150	$150	$150	$150
$150	$150	$150	$150	$150	$200	$200
$200	$200	$200	$200	$200	$200	$250
$250	$250	$250	$250	$250	$250	$250
$250	$300	$300	$300	$300	$300	$300
$350	$350	$350				

Notes:

$10,000 in 52 Weeks Savings Challenge

$100	$100	$100	$100	$100	$100	$100
$100	$100	$100	$100	$100	$150	$150
$150	$150	$150	$150	$150	$150	$150
$150	$150	$150	$150	$150	$200	$200
$200	$200	$200	$200	$200	$200	$250
$250	$250	$250	$250	$250	$250	$250
$250	$300	$300	$300	$300	$300	$300
$350	$350	$350				

Notes:

$10,000 in 52 Weeks
Savings Challenge

$100	$100	$100	$100	$100	$100	$100
$100	$100	$100	$100	$100	$150	$150
$150	$150	$150	$150	$150	$150	$150
$150	$150	$150	$150	$150	$200	$200
$200	$200	$200	$200	$200	$200	$250
$250	$250	$250	$250	$250	$250	$250
$250	$300	$300	$300	$300	$300	$300
$350	$350	$350				

Notes:

$15,000 in 6 Months

Ultimate Savings Challenge

$125	$125	$125	$125	$125	$125	$125
$125	$125	$125	$150	$150	$150	$150
$150	$150	$150	$150	$150	$150	$175
$175	$175	$175	$175	$175	$175	$175
$175	$175	$200	$200	$200	$200	$200
$200	$200	$200	$200	$200	$225	$225
$225	$225	$225	$225	$225	$225	$225
$225	$275	$275	$275	$275	$275	$275
$275	$275	$275	$275	$350	$350	$350
$350	$350	$350	$350	$350	$350	$350

Notes:

$15,000 in 6 Months

Ultimate Savings Challenge

$125	$125	$125	$125	$125	$125	$125
$125	$125	$125	$150	$150	$150	$150
$150	$150	$150	$150	$150	$150	$175
$175	$175	$175	$175	$175	$175	$175
$175	$175	$200	$200	$200	$200	$200
$200	$200	$200	$200	$200	$225	$225
$225	$225	$225	$225	$225	$225	$225
$225	$275	$275	$275	$275	$275	$275
$275	$275	$275	$275	$350	$350	$350
$350	$350	$350	$350	$350	$350	$350

Notes:

$15,000 in 6 Months

Ultimate Savings Challenge

$125	$125	$125	$125	$125	$125	$125
$125	$125	$125	$150	$150	$150	$150
$150	$150	$150	$150	$150	$150	$175
$175	$175	$175	$175	$175	$175	$175
$175	$175	$200	$200	$200	$200	$200
$200	$200	$200	$200	$200	$225	$225
$225	$225	$225	$225	$225	$225	$225
$225	$275	$275	$275	$275	$275	$275
$275	$275	$275	$275	$350	$350	$350
$350	$350	$350	$350	$350	$350	$350

Notes: _____

$15,000 in 6 Months

Ultimate Savings Challenge

$125	$125	$125	$125	$125	$125	$125
$125	$125	$125	$150	$150	$150	$150
$150	$150	$150	$150	$150	$150	$175
$175	$175	$175	$175	$175	$175	$175
$175	$175	$200	$200	$200	$200	$200
$200	$200	$200	$200	$200	$225	$225
$225	$225	$225	$225	$225	$225	$225
$225	$275	$275	$275	$275	$275	$275
$275	$275	$275	$275	$350	$350	$350
$350	$350	$350	$350	$350	$350	$350

Notes: _____
_____

$15,000 in 6 Months

Ultimate Savings Challenge

$125	$125	$125	$125	$125	$125	$125
$125	$125	$125	$150	$150	$150	$150
$150	$150	$150	$150	$150	$150	$175
$175	$175	$175	$175	$175	$175	$175
$175	$175	$200	$200	$200	$200	$200
$200	$200	$200	$200	$200	$225	$225
$225	$225	$225	$225	$225	$225	$225
$225	$275	$275	$275	$275	$275	$275
$275	$275	$275	$275	$350	$350	$350
$350	$350	$350	$350	$350	$350	$350

Notes:

$15,000 in 6 Months

Ultimate Savings Challenge

$125	$125	$125	$125	$125	$125	$125
$125	$125	$125	$150	$150	$150	$150
$150	$150	$150	$150	$150	$150	$175
$175	$175	$175	$175	$175	$175	$175
$175	$175	$200	$200	$200	$200	$200
$200	$200	$200	$200	$200	$225	$225
$225	$225	$225	$225	$225	$225	$225
$225	$275	$275	$275	$275	$275	$275
$275	$275	$275	$275	$350	$350	$350
$350	$350	$350	$350	$350	$350	$350

Notes:

$15,000 in 6 Months

Ultimate Savings Challenge

$125	$125	$125	$125	$125	$125	$125
$125	$125	$125	$150	$150	$150	$150
$150	$150	$150	$150	$150	$150	$175
$175	$175	$175	$175	$175	$175	$175
$175	$175	$200	$200	$200	$200	$200
$200	$200	$200	$200	$200	$225	$225
$225	$225	$225	$225	$225	$225	$225
$225	$275	$275	$275	$275	$275	$275
$275	$275	$275	$275	$350	$350	$350
$350	$350	$350	$350	$350	$350	$350

Notes: _____

$15,000 in 6 Months

Ultimate Savings Challenge

$125	$125	$125	$125	$125	$125	$125
$125	$125	$125	$150	$150	$150	$150
$150	$150	$150	$150	$150	$150	$175
$175	$175	$175	$175	$175	$175	$175
$175	$175	$200	$200	$200	$200	$200
$200	$200	$200	$200	$200	$225	$225
$225	$225	$225	$225	$225	$225	$225
$225	$275	$275	$275	$275	$275	$275
$275	$275	$275	$275	$350	$350	$350
$350	$350	$350	$350	$350	$350	$350

Notes:

$15,000 in 6 Months

Ultimate Savings Challenge

$125	$125	$125	$125	$125	$125	$125
$125	$125	$125	$150	$150	$150	$150
$150	$150	$150	$150	$150	$150	$175
$175	$175	$175	$175	$175	$175	$175
$175	$175	$200	$200	$200	$200	$200
$200	$200	$200	$200	$200	$225	$225
$225	$225	$225	$225	$225	$225	$225
$225	$275	$275	$275	$275	$275	$275
$275	$275	$275	$275	$350	$350	$350
$350	$350	$350	$350	$350	$350	$350

Notes: _____

$15,000 in 6 Months

Ultimate Savings Challenge

$125	$125	$125	$125	$125	$125	$125
$125	$125	$125	$150	$150	$150	$150
$150	$150	$150	$150	$150	$150	$175
$175	$175	$175	$175	$175	$175	$175
$175	$175	$200	$200	$200	$200	$200
$200	$200	$200	$200	$200	$225	$225
$225	$225	$225	$225	$225	$225	$225
$225	$275	$275	$275	$275	$275	$275
$275	$275	$275	$275	$350	$350	$350
$350	$350	$350	$350	$350	$350	$350

Notes: _____

$15,000 in 6 Months

Ultimate Savings Challenge

$125	$125	$125	$125	$125	$125	$125
$125	$125	$125	$150	$150	$150	$150
$150	$150	$150	$150	$150	$150	$175
$175	$175	$175	$175	$175	$175	$175
$175	$175	$200	$200	$200	$200	$200
$200	$200	$200	$200	$200	$225	$225
$225	$225	$225	$225	$225	$225	$225
$225	$275	$275	$275	$275	$275	$275
$275	$275	$275	$275	$350	$350	$350
$350	$350	$350	$350	$350	$350	$350

Notes:

$15,000 in 6 Months

Ultimate Savings Challenge

$125	$125	$125	$125	$125	$125	$125
$125	$125	$125	$150	$150	$150	$150
$150	$150	$150	$150	$150	$150	$175
$175	$175	$175	$175	$175	$175	$175
$175	$175	$200	$200	$200	$200	$200
$200	$200	$200	$200	$200	$225	$225
$225	$225	$225	$225	$225	$225	$225
$225	$275	$275	$275	$275	$275	$275
$275	$275	$275	$275	$350	$350	$350
$350	$350	$350	$350	$350	$350	$350

Notes:

$15,000 in 6 Months

Ultimate Savings Challenge

$125	$125	$125	$125	$125	$125	$125
$125	$125	$125	$150	$150	$150	$150
$150	$150	$150	$150	$150	$150	$175
$175	$175	$175	$175	$175	$175	$175
$175	$175	$200	$200	$200	$200	$200
$200	$200	$200	$200	$200	$225	$225
$225	$225	$225	$225	$225	$225	$225
$225	$275	$275	$275	$275	$275	$275
$275	$275	$275	$275	$350	$350	$350
$350	$350	$350	$350	$350	$350	$350

Notes:

$15,000 in 6 Months

Ultimate Savings Challenge

$125	$125	$125	$125	$125	$125	$125
$125	$125	$125	$150	$150	$150	$150
$150	$150	$150	$150	$150	$150	$175
$175	$175	$175	$175	$175	$175	$175
$175	$175	$200	$200	$200	$200	$200
$200	$200	$200	$200	$200	$225	$225
$225	$225	$225	$225	$225	$225	$225
$225	$275	$275	$275	$275	$275	$275
$275	$275	$275	$275	$350	$350	$350
$350	$350	$350	$350	$350	$350	$350

Notes: _____

$15,000 in 6 Months

Ultimate savings Challenge

$125	$125	$125	$125	$125	$125	$125
$125	$125	$125	$150	$150	$150	$150
$150	$150	$150	$150	$150	$150	$175
$175	$175	$175	$175	$175	$175	$175
$175	$175	$200	$200	$200	$200	$200
$200	$200	$200	$200	$200	$225	$225
$225	$225	$225	$225	$225	$225	$225
$225	$275	$275	$275	$275	$275	$275
$275	$275	$275	$275	$350	$350	$350
$350	$350	$350	$350	$350	$350	$350

Notes: